Measuring the Effectiveness of Special Operations

LINDA ROBINSON, DANIEL EGEL, RYAN ANDREW BROWN

RAND ARROYO CENTER

Prepared for the United States Army
Approved for public release; distribution unlimited

For more information on this publication, visit www.rand.org/t/RR2504

Library of Congress Cataloging-in-Publication Data is available for this publication.
ISBN: 978-1-9774-0174-8

Published by the RAND Corporation, Santa Monica, Calif.

Preface

This report documents research and analysis conducted as part of a project entitled Special Operations Forces (SOF) Measures of Effectiveness, sponsored by U.S. Army Special Operations Command. The purpose of the project was to develop a system of metric-capture and evidence-based assessments to evaluate the success (or failure) of various special operations missions and demonstrate how Army special operations forces contribute to theater and national security objectives. A companion volume—Linda Robinson, Daniel Egel, and Ryan Andrew Brown, *Measuring the Effectiveness of Special Operations: Appendixes*, Santa Monica, Calif.: RAND Corporation, RR-2504/1-A, 2019—provides the appendixes.

This research was conducted within RAND Arroyo Center's Strategy, Doctrine, and Resources Program. RAND Arroyo Center, part of the RAND Corporation, is a federally funded research and development center (FFRDC) sponsored by the United States Army.

RAND operates under a "Federal-Wide Assurance" (FWA00003425) and complies with the *Code of Federal Regulations for the Protection of Human Subjects Under United States Law* (45 CFR 46), also known as "the Common Rule," as well as with the implementation guidance set forth in DoD Instruction 3216.02. As applicable, this compliance includes reviews and approvals by RAND's Institutional Review Board (the Human Subjects Protection Committee) and by the U.S. Army. The views of sources utilized in this study are solely their own and do not represent the official policy or position of DoD or the U.S. Government.

Contents

Figures, Tables, and Boxes

Figures

Tables

Boxes

Summary

This report provides a methodology for evidence-based assessment of operational-level special operations forces (SOF) headquarters. The goals of our proposed operational-level methodology are to offer a rigorous and objective assessment that provides the commander and staff with information that can enhance the effectiveness of operations and to justify continued funding of operations (if warranted by assessment results). Our assessment approach is designed to address both the general challenges (e.g., establishing causality) and the SOF-specific challenges (e.g., dynamic environment, limited budget) inherent in conducting assessments.

Two core innovations underlie our assessment approach. The first is recognizing the importance of integrating personnel across the SOF enterprise in the assessment process. The detailed daily data that tactical elements across the SOF enterprise collect during operations—which we call *operational data* and includes situation reports (SITREPs), intelligence reports, and concepts of operations, among others—offer a potentially powerful, longitudinal data source for assessments. These granular data are particularly important for assessment of SOF operations because the unique SOF mission set and dynamic environments in which SOF operates dramatically attenuate the effectiveness of top-down and centralized assessment processes. Thus, a secondary goal of this report is to provide an assessment methodology that is accessible to operators across the SOF enterprise because their efforts will be integral to the success of operational-level assessments of SOF.

The second innovation is recognizing the value of exploiting *ambient data*, which includes individuals' digital fingerprints (e.g., social media and other digital communication), satellite-based imagery (e.g., movement, agricultural production), and traditional media (e.g., newspapers). These data provide an objective and longitudinal tool for measuring morale among partner forces, enemy elements, and civilian populations; evaluating changes in economic activity or movements of people; and assessing perceptions. Ambient data can be collected systematically in both permissive and denied environments, a characteristic that is crucial for assessments in the environments in which SOF operates.

We used multiple methods to develop the standardized assessment process for operational-level SOF headquarters in this report. The first was a detailed review of a dozen SOF efforts of durations longer than one year—many of which one or more of the authors had been personally involved in assessing—to describe how these long-duration missions are organized and how they were assessed. The second was a detailed review of existing doctrine, assessments of military operations (both publicly available and not), and assessments being conducted by development professionals. The third, which was designed to describe potential emerging assessment techniques that SOF might consider, was a series of consultations with relevant private sector enterprises. Finally, we conducted a limited objective exercise involving senior-level representatives from across the Army SOF enterprise and the theater special operations commands to discuss, validate, and update the assessment approach emerging from the three previous activities.

A Line of Effort–Based Assessment Approach

Line of effort (LOE)–based approaches are now common for strategic- and operational-level assessments of military operations. Such an approach is particularly appropriate for SOF operational-level assessments because the objectives that SOF aims to achieve are commonly articulated in operational plans specifying multiple LOEs that are executed through SOF core activities and capabilities.

Our assessment approach is designed around the four LOEs that underpin the vast majority of operations conducted by SOF operational-level headquarters. *Develop, enable, and employ partner forces* includes the recruitment, training, equipping, advising, and sustainment of partner forces, including both state and nonstate actors. *Precision targeting* is the use of both direct action and counternetwork activities to degrade or suppress enemy forces, which can either eliminate a specific threat or create time and space for other operations. *Influence via military information support operations* influence the attitudes and behaviors of key individuals or populations—including the enemy, partner forces, and civilians—using a diverse range of media and related tools. *Influence via civil affairs operations* identifies and mitigates underlying causes of instability within civil society, thus enhancing the legitimacy of a governing entity and limiting the freedom of maneuver for enemy elements. These LOEs are not the only ones used in campaigns, of course, and it should be noted that influence can be exercised via other types of operations.

A key component of an LOE-based assessment approach for SOF is the careful development of measures of effectiveness (MOEs), which are designed to help gauge whether objectives are being obtained, for each of the LOEs. Our assessment approach team used a four-step process to develop MOEs, based on the approach recommended in joint doctrine for selecting these MOEs: (1) identify effects associated with the objective of each LOE; (2) brainstorm a wide variety of MOEs; (3) evaluate the list of MOEs based on their relevance, measurability, malleability, and distinctness; and (4) identify data and indicators that can be used for tracking progress for each MOE. This process focused primarily on operational and ambient data (discussed earlier) because collecting assessment-specific data (e.g., polling conducted by local nationals) is both resource intensive and difficult in nonpermissive environments.

Seven-Step Assessment Process

Our assessment process—which we illustrate using a fictional operational-level SOF headquarters deploying to Atropia, the Special Operations Joint Task Force–Atropia—is divided into seven sequential steps. The central goal of the assessment process is to demonstrate how assessment teams can collect the needed data and both select and implement the appropriate analytical technique. Quantitative and qualitative methodologies can produce results with causal interpretations, and the type of data available determines the appropriate method.

Figure S.1 outlines the seven steps in our proposed assessment method, which should be integrated into both the planning and commander's decisionmaking cycle. The details of this seven-step process should be developed before deployment and refined to reflect the commander's vision; we recommend conducting assessments quarterly during the campaign. Predeployment preparation increases efficiency and objectivity and allows the assessment team to arrange for assistance from U.S.-based commands or other higher headquarters.

Figure S.1
Seven Steps of Special Operations Forces Operational-Level Assessment

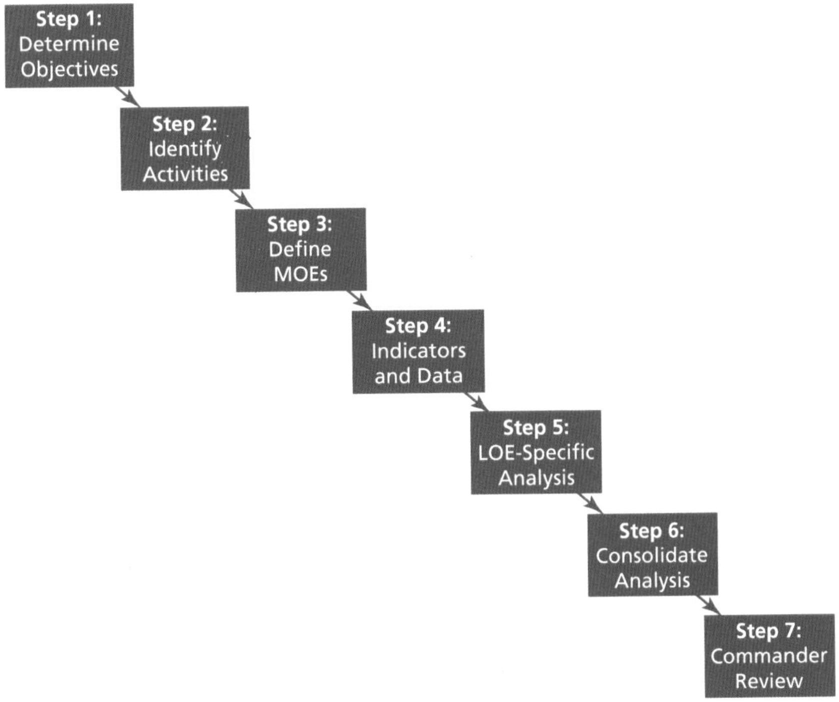

An assessment process cannot be successful unless the entire deployed SOF team understands its utility. In the first instance, assessment is a means of providing the commander with a rigorous, unbiased picture of the effects being achieved and not achieved, informing deliberations over what adaptations are required. The participation of the entire SOF team enables it to offer insights as part of a collaborative effort. Finally, involving the entire SOF team will ensure that the assessment cell receives the needed operational data and cooperation from all echelons. Knowing where efforts are producing results and where they are falling short will enable the commander to choose the best possible road at any given juncture.

We describe the seven steps as follows:

- **Step 1: Determine objectives.** Identify the key LOEs and the objectives of each from a review of official documentation (e.g., operational plans) and consultation with both planners and the commander. This includes developing specific thresholds (expectations for time, number of operations, or other metrics to achieve objectives, intermediate military objectives, or specific effects). Work with the planners and commander to ensure that the objectives are specific, measurable, achievable, relevant, and time bound. The LOEs and the constituent activities represent the *ways* that the plan envisions achieving objectives.
- **Step 2: Identify activities.** Develop a *mission tracker* that collates details on all relevant activities—all activities that might influence any of the LOEs and associated objectives—of the components of the operational-level headquarters. The mission tracker should be based on data provided regularly in a standardized SITREP. This step should also articulate the theory of change or logic model that explicitly spells out how the activities grouped under each LOE are to achieve the desired objectives.
- **Step 3: Define MOEs.** Select MOEs, starting with the standardized list and grounding in operational context, noting specific thresholds and time horizons for effects. Ensure that the MOEs are specific, measurable, achievable, relevant, and time bound.

- **Step 4: Develop indicators and collect data.** Develop a set of indicators based on available data streams. Indicators that can be codified into operational data and those that can be derived from ambient data are preferred.
- **Step 5: Conduct LOE-specific analysis.** Select the appropriate analytical technique for the available data and conduct the analysis. When all data are quantifiable and when SOF activities are conducted in many different areas or with many different units (more than 50), it is preferable to use quantitative methods with causal interpretations—specifically, multivariate panel regression. Qualitative methods with causal interpretations—specifically, process tracing—are appropriate only when the number of units of analysis is limited or when some critical data are not quantifiable. One of the core analytic tasks is to detect change over time (i.e., from a baseline) that is plausibly linked with SOF activities.
- **Step 6: Consolidate analysis.** The LOE-specific results should be presented in a combined manner to facilitate visualization of how the plan's LOEs are or are not progressing.
- **Step 7: Commander review.** Review the results with the commander. The results should enable him to adjust LOEs or activities or other inputs to improve outputs and outcomes. The assessment process including MOEs may need to be adjusted to provide the desired granularity, periodicity, and fidelity.

Overcoming the Unique Challenges for Operational-Level Assessment of Special Operations

An accurate and defensible assessment of SOF must first overcome the challenges all assessments of military operations face: establishing a result that is plausibly causal, measuring the complex types of effects that these operations are trying to achieve without resorting to "junk arithmetic," and ensuring that the analysis is sufficiently timely to support decisionmaking without being disruptive to operations. In addition, an effective assessment of SOF must reflect the unique difficulty of measuring effects achieved through partner forces and must be sufficiently flexible to capture the dynamic nature of special operations, robust to the fact that SOF effects are achieved in denied environments and often in the realm of attitude and affect, and able to account for the synergies of SOF efforts across LOEs.

Our approach for addressing these challenges relies on novel and creative ways of exploiting the unique types of data available to SOF. For one, operational data—the data that the operational-level headquarters and its subordinate elements *already* produce—are critical for our assessment approach. These data provide highly granular information on the types of activities the operational-level headquarters is involved in and offer a unique perspective on environmental factors that can function as indicators for many SOF MOEs. Developing a standardized tactical-level SITREP and collating information collected by headquarters' staff sections can create a powerful tool for supporting assessments.

New technological capabilities have allowed the world to generate, store, and share more data each year than can feasibly be analyzed—even with rapidly advancing computational means for making sense of large quantities of unstructured data. But this also provides new data sources that can be exploited for SOF operational assessment. Despite the proliferation of new ways to ingest, visualize, and analyze social media data, it is important to keep two caveats in mind. First, country-level protections (as in China), corporate privacy protections, and individual countermeasures are increasingly restricting access to social media data. Second, individual social media platforms provide only a limited slice of the total sphere of human interaction. Despite these challenges, social media data present a unique opportunity to view real-world and real-time organization of social movements, interactions among adversaries and collaborators, and reactions to events in conflict-ridden areas.

In concert with the expansion of data sources, a suite of new developments in computational analysis promises to affect SOF assessment practices. Computational text analysis allows the user to analyze more text than human beings can usefully read. In analysis of social media data sets, text analysis can be combined with social network analysis to examine how communities that interact with each other show distinct linguistic signatures. New developments in *reso-*

nance analysis use statistical techniques to model the spread of specific linguistic signatures through networks and can be used to gauge the impact of military information support operations (psychological operations [PSYOP]) or enemy propaganda. Additionally, a large percentage of military operational data (e.g., SITREPs) comes in the form of semistructured or unstructured text and is therefore amenable to computational text analysis. Finally, nontextual data are now amenable to machine-learning and artificial-intelligence approaches for classification and analysis. While analytic tools for images, audio, and video are in their infancy, this promises to open up an additional treasure trove of data and insights into the cognitive states, emotions, and communication of SOF enemies and host-nation populations.

SOF-specific operations are frequently either focused on preventing conflict or maintaining a steady state. This creates unique challenges for assessments because measuring effectiveness may require multiyear assessments or necessitate proving that SOF operations prevented the emergence of instability (i.e., proving a "negative" result). For these types of operations, modifying assessment approaches created by development and law enforcement professionals—which typically require assessment updates at one-year intervals and involve both quantitative and qualitative analysis, akin to the triangulation approach that we recommend—for application to the LOEs of special operations is likely to be most effective.

Implementing the SOF operational assessment approach recommended in this report will require steps across the spectrum of doctrine, organization, training, material, leadership development and education, personnel, facilities, and policy. Implementation will include incorporating the approach into doctrine and training and having the organizational dedication to standing up an assessment cell. Sufficient facilities and material support—including access to data streams and appropriate analytic platforms and reachback support—is vital as well.

Acknowledgments

We are indebted to many representatives of the special operations community who supported this effort. The U.S. Army Special Operations Command (USASOC) commanding general believed that rigorous, rapid assessments would greatly enhance special operations forces (SOF) operations and the ability to demonstrate whether, when, and to what degree they are achieving the intended effects. He provided critical guidance throughout the project. Other Army SOF commanders provided invaluable advice and support during a day-long limited objective experiment to test the incipient approach. We owe thanks as well to many other individuals throughout the SOF community who provided insights from their own research and experience and participated in our exercise. We are especially indebted to the theater special operations commands that sent one or more delegates to attend our limited objective exercise—and that provided considerable substantive inputs to this report. The USASOC Commander's Initiative Group and USASOC G-9 Studies Section provided tireless logistical and intellectual support throughout this project.

We would also like to extend thanks to RAND Corporation colleagues Eric Robinson and Isaac Baruffi for their important efforts on this project. In addition, RAND assessment experts Christopher Paul and Patrick Johnston provided important early critiques to our approach. Joshua Mendelsohn, Madeline Magnuson, William Marcellino, Elizabeth Bodine-Baron, and Zev Winkelman provided essential consultation and analysis on social media, social networks, and text analysis. We benefited enormously from the detailed peer reviews of Christopher Paul of RAND and David Maxwell of Georgetown University. This report draws on the substantial body of research on assessment methods produced by many of our RAND colleagues, including notable work by Paul. Finally, we thank Sally Sleeper, director of RAND Arroyo Center's Strategy, Doctrine, and Resources program, for her substantive input and leadership and the many RAND Arroyo Center and RAND Publishing staff members who play crucial roles in bringing every project to fruition.

CHAPTER ONE

Introduction

In the current resource-constrained environment, it is imperative that the U.S. Army be able to provide accurate and defensible evaluations of the effectiveness of its special operations forces (SOF). Currently, assessments are not standardized or consistently implemented across the SOF enterprise. Furthermore, doctrinal recommendations for assessment need to be adjusted for SOF's frequently small footprint and staffing. The ability to ascertain whether or not SOF operations are resulting in progress toward specified objectives will both enhance the efficacy of these efforts and facilitate SOF efforts to effectively advocate for continued funding of operations (if warranted by assessment results), by providing commanders with timely and relevant information on the efficacy of their operations.

This report provides a methodology for evidence-based assessments of operational-level SOF headquarters. Our assessment methodology is rigorous and objective, is appropriate for the uniqueness of SOF operations, provides sufficiently frequent feedback guide operational-level decisionmaking, and is replicable and scalable.

This chapter describes the process that we used to develop the assessment methodology in this report. We begin by describing a set of general requirements for assessments of an operational-level SOF headquarters, comparing and contrasting these requirements to assessments recommended in joint doctrine for larger formations. The two subsequent sections describe how our assessment approach is designed to overcome the general and SOF-specific challenges facing assessment. The fourth section then outlines the approach used for developing this report, and a final section reviews the overall organization of this report, which is designed to provide operators across the SOF enterprise with an accessible tool for developing and implementing assessments across their diverse range of operations.

Requirements for a SOF-Specific Operational Assessment

A SOF operational-level assessment is comparable to other assessments of military formations in its primary goals: It must provide the commander, staff, and other stakeholders needed information about conditions on the ground to "inform decisions about the future and make operations effective."[1] The assessment should provide feedback on what is working (and what is not) to support ongoing decisionmaking on the appropriate disposition of forces, needed orders, and plan development.[2] It must therefore be fully integrated into both operational planning and the commander's decisionmaking cycle.[3] To support operational-level decisionmaking, the assessment must focus on answering the question of whether the command is "doing the right things," typically referred to as *measures of effectiveness* (MOEs), rather

---

[1] Army Techniques Publication (ATP) 5-0.3, Marine Corps Reference Publication 5-1C, Navy Tactics, Techniques, and Procedures 5-01.3, Air Force Tactics, Techniques, and Procedures 3-2.87, *Operation Assessment: Multi-Service Tactics, Techniques, and Procedures for Operation Assessment*, Air Land Sea Application Center, August 2015, p. 5.

[2] Army Doctrine Reference Publication (ADRP) 5-0, *The Operations Process*, Washington, D.C.: Headquarters, Department of the Army, 2012, p. 2-2. ATP 5-0.3, 2015, p. 6, similarly describes operational assessment as "a continuous process to determine the overall effectiveness of employing joint force capabilities during military operations by measuring the progress toward accomplishing a task, creating a condition or effect, or achieving an objective that supports decision making to make operations more effective."

[3] U.S. Army War College, *Campaign Planning Handbook*, Carlisle Barracks, Pa.: Department of Military Strategy, Planning, and Operations, 2016; ATP 5-0.3, 2015. For SOF-specific guidance on assessment and its relationship to operational decisionmaking, see Gittipong Paruchabutr, Christopher Parapone, Geoffrey Demarest, Grant Martin, Christopher Kirk, Cody Brown, Curtis Clayton, William Harris, Thomas Heilman, and Brian Kaiser, *SOF Campaign Planner's Handbook of Operational Art and Design*, Fort Bragg, N.C.: U.S. Army Special Operations Command, September 16, 2014.

than simply assessing "doing things right."[4] The assessments should also be designed to satisfy the information requirements of national-level authorities (e.g., a combatant command, Congress).

The requirements for a SOF operational-level assessment will depend on resource constraints and the unique SOF mission set. Joint doctrine recommends a multinodal assessment cell—with an assessment chief, a data management cell, a survey cell, and an analysis cell[5]—and recommended assessment frameworks can involve evaluating hundreds of separate metrics.[6] However, given the small staff of SOF operational-level headquarters, even the largest SOF assessment teams are likely to consist of only a handful of individuals.[7] The assessment approach must thus work efficiently to help inform the joint task force or global combatant command of how SOF activities fit with higher headquarters' objectives and effects. This requires an enterprise solution in which tactical and operational SOF elements work collaboratively to produce the best assessment possible. In addition to overcoming the challenges common to all assessments of operational headquarters, the unique SOF mission set involves overcoming a set of additional challenges—these two sets of challenges, and how our

---

4 *Measures of performance* (MOPs) are used for assessing whether things are "being done right," which is discussed in greater detail in Chapters Three and Four. For a more detailed discussion of MOEs and MOPs, see Deployable Training Division, *Insights and Best Practices Focus Paper: Design and Planning*, Suffolk, Va.: Joint Staff J7, 2013, p. 3. Note that excessive focus on identifying the differences between MOPs and MOEs can be distracting because there is no clear dividing line and—depending on the level of focus for the assessment (both time and geographic scope)—an MOP in one context might be an MOE in another.

5 Joint Doctrine Note (JDN) 1-15, *Operation Assessment*, Washington, D.C.: Joint Staff, January 15, 2015.

6 As an example, the Measuring Progress in Conflict Environments framework, which was developed as a partnership between the U.S. Department of Defense and the U.S. interagency community to measure "progress of stabilization and reconstruction missions in conflict environments," includes some 800 unique metrics (Joint Staff, *Commander's Handbook for Assessment Planning and Execution*, Vers. 1.0, Suffolk, Va.: Joint Staff J-7, Joint and Coalition Warfighting, September 9, 2011, p. II-13).

7 As an example, even the well-resourced Special Operations Joint Task Force (SOJTF) Afghanistan only had a five-person assessment team, and many of these individuals had one if not multiple other duties.

assessment approach overcomes them, is the focus of the next two sections.

Addressing General Assessment Challenges

Our assessment approach, while structured to accommodate the resourcing constraints of SOF operational-level headquarters, is designed to address the major challenges for all types of operational-level assessments that are also relevant for SOF assessment. In the following paragraphs, we introduce these four types of challenges, and the remainder of this section discusses how our assessment approach addresses each.[8]

A challenge all types of assessments face is *establishing a plausibly causal relationship* between activities and effects.[9] This challenge—often described by the aphorism "correlation does not imply causation"[10]—is particularly insidious in assessment of military operations, which are typically conducted in dynamic settings where other stakeholders (e.g., interagency actors, international community, host-nation elements, enemy forces) are also actively trying to influence those same outcomes. This makes it difficult to assess whether success (or failure) was due to SOF activities or due to the efforts of other stakeholders.[11] This challenge is particularly relevant for outcomes related to "human

---

8 We identified these four challenges first by conducting a literature search on operational assessments, focused on SOF and SOF-like activities and then by participating in briefings and other interactions with U.S. Army Special Operations Command (USASOC) and other SOF personnel to first expand, then merge and focus the description of general assessment challenges and ensure that they are relevant for SOF operational-level assessment.

9 See David Freedman, "From Association to Causation: Some Remarks on the History of Statistics," *Statistical Science*, Vol. 14, No. 3, August 1999, for a discussion.

10 For example, Ben Connable, *Embracing the Fog of War: Assessment and Metrics in Counterinsurgency*, Santa Monica, Calif.: RAND Corporation, MG-1086-DOD, 2012.

11 In a worst case, this may "devolve into simply gauging the environment, with little understanding as to how changes in that environment are the result of military activities." (Leo J. Blanken and Jason J. Lepore, "Principals, Agents, and Assessment," in Leo J. Blanken, Hy Rothstein, and Jason J. Lepore, eds., *Assessing War: The Challenge of Measuring Success and Failure*, Washington, D.C.: Georgetown University Press, 2015, p. 8).

behavior, attitudes, and perception,"[12] which frequently are the focus of SOF activities (as described in Chapter Two) and can create significant challenges for collecting appropriate data. This challenge is of foremost importance in our context because understanding the effects of operations is central to effective decisionmaking by an operational-level commander.

Three other major challenges affect assessments of military operations. Prominent among these are challenges of *measurement*, in that the types of factors that military operations are trying to influence (e.g., underlying support for enemy forces among host nationals, operational capability of a partnered unit) cannot easily be measured directly based on existing data;[13] this challenge sometimes leads to simplified quantification of qualitative data or "junk arithmetic."[14] Another class of challenges relates to the assessment *process* itself. The process of assessment may induce potentially undesirable behavior among the operators being assessed because they may begin to operate to achieve metrics rather than the intended outcomes.[15] In addition, the assessors may shade their assessments, even unconsciously, if the commander

[12] Deployable Training Division, 2013, p. 1.

[13] Assessments of military operations frequently employ available data (see data discussion in Chapter Four as a proxy for the effect they want to measure, which can create misleading results (e.g., Daniel Egel and Peter Glick, *Assessing the Stabilizing Effects of Development Programming: A Review of USAID's Evaluation Efforts in Afghanistan*, Santa Monica, Calif.: RAND Corporation, WR-1106-MSI, 2016). Recognizing this challenge, another recommendation is to "not ignore data that are hard, but necessary, to measure. Report them early in the planning process to the commander. Not allocating collection resources to necessary measures puts the assessment quality at risk, and the commander needs to decide whether to accept that risk, reallocate resources to collection, or adjust the assessment plan" (ATP 5-0.3, 2015, p. 21).

[14] For a discussion of this challenge and ways to rigorously convert qualitative to quantitative data in military assessments, see William P. Upshur, Jonathon W. Roginski, and David J. Kilcullen, "Recognizing Systems in Afghanistan: Lessons Learned and New Approaches to Operational Assessments," *Prism*, Vol. 3, No. 3, June 2012.

[15] For example, Robert B. Sotire, "Measuring Performance and Effectiveness in Irregular Warfare: Preventing Dysfunctional Behavior," Newport, R.I.: Naval War College, 2009.

does not stress the need for strict impartiality of the assessment.[16] The *timeliness* of assessments is a final challenge,[17] and failure to integrate assessments into both the planning and the execution of military operations hampers the overall effectiveness of assessments in recent military operations.[18] There is an inherent tension between rigor and real-time feedback because the types of automated analysis required for real-time feedback can be too coarse and insufficiently contextualized to support effective decisionmaking.[19]

Our assessment approach—which is detailed in Chapter Four and illustrated in Chapter Five—is specifically designed with these four challenges in mind. Three core characteristics of our proposed approach help address the *causality* challenge. First, our assessment

---

[16] Operational headquarters are typically incentivized to produce overly optimistic assessments for external audiences:

> Assessments that reflect bottom-up data collection and analysis, while ostensibly objective, risk creating dissatisfaction among higher leadership if the results do not show sufficient progress. As a consequence, unlike the skeptical approach commanders often take to assessments in the planning process, those delivered "up and out" to policymakers often reflect an optimism that is either not present in or even counter to internal, bottom-up assessments. (Emily Mushen and Jonathan Schroden, *Are We Winning? A Brief History of Military Operations Assessment*, Washington, D.C.: CNA, September 2014, p. 36)

[17] Successful assessment integration into the operations process gives commanders a means of proactively identifying and adjusting to emerging opportunities and risks to mission accomplishment. Timely recognition of opportunities and risks affords commanders a distinct advantage, possibly allowing them to catch the enemy off balance and rapidly end a battle; refocus joint force capabilities to minimize disruption; or hasten accomplishment of objectives, conditions, and end states. Conversely, missed opportunities and risks result in protracted engagements, higher casualties, increased potential for tactical defeat, and operational and strategic setback (ATP 5-0.3, 2015, p. ix).

[18] The challenge of timeliness has been identified as a "contributing factor" in what has been described as an overall lack of success of assessments in recent military operations, with the "few documented successes . . . achieved only after much effort and revision" (ATP 5-0.3, p. ix). This document attributes the challenge to a "a lack of doctrine providing guidance and discussion of the practical activity necessary to integrate assessment into the operations process" (ATP 5-0.3).

[19] Mushen and Schroden highlight that this challenge of "meeting expectations of modern audiences without compromising the integrity of the assessment may prove even more challenging in the future" (Mushen and Schroden, 2014, p. 37).

focuses on data sources that can provide detailed longitudinal data on both SOF activities and their desired effects—specifically, we propose that existing operational data (e.g., situation reports [SITREPs], intelligence reporting) and ambient data feeds (e.g., social media, satellite imagery) should be a central component of SOF assessments. Second, the availability of these detailed longitudinal data allows the assessment team to use analytical approaches that academics widely use to provide causally defensible results—these include both *quasi-experimental multivariate panel regression*, a widely used quantitative technique, and *process tracing*, a qualitative technique that produces similarly defensible results.[20] Third, our approach is designed so that every desired effect is measured using multiple data sources and analytical methodologies, which we call *triangulation*.[21] Triangulation gives causally defensible results only if either the qualitative or quantitative methods themselves give these results. The employment of qualitative and quantitative data and analytic methods affords the greatest likelihood for a successful causal analysis by allowing the assessor to cross-validate the findings from each analytical approach.

Our assessment addresses the challenge of *measurement* by leveraging emerging technologies that make analysis of ambient data—social media and other pattern-of-life data—feasible. The *process* challenge is mitigated by fully integrating the assessment process into both planning and operations at all levels, so that any behavior induced by the assessment is deliberate. This integration also allows our proposed approach to mitigate the *timeliness* challenge. Chapters Four and Five introduce the use of emerging technologies to analyze ambient data

---

[20] Multivariate analysis is based on the statistical principle of multivariate statistics, which involves observation and analysis of more than one statistical outcome variable at a time. Multivariate regression is a technique that estimates a single regression model with more than one outcome variable. Panel (data) analysis is a statistical method, widely used in social science, epidemiology, and econometrics to analyze two-dimensional (typically, cross-sectional and longitudinal) panel data. The data are usually collected over time and over the same individuals and then a regression is run over these two dimensions. Quasi-experimental design is used when a true experimental design with a control group is not feasible. The validity of quasi-experimental research can be improved by specific methods that assist in identifying a comparison group, controlling bias, and using appropriate statistical analyses.

[21] In the academic literature, this is called either *triangulation* or *mixed methods*.

and the integration of operational data into the assessment process, which Chapter Six discusses more fully.

Addressing SOF-Specific Assessment Challenges

Our approach is also designed to overcome a number of SOF-specific challenges to assessment. First, many of the effects that SOF is trying to achieve are indirect, with *effects achieved through a partner force*, as discussed in Chapter Two. Measuring the effectiveness of partner forces is notoriously difficult, given the difficulty of collecting reliable data on partner forces and given the importance of indicators that are inherently subjective—e.g., partner will or morale—and thus difficult to measure objectively.[22] It is equally challenging to determine whether and to what degree the SOF activities contributed to the effects partners achieve.

Second, SOF operations typically require *flexibility*—constant operational "improvisation and adaptation" by both tactical- and operational-level elements[23]—given the complex and rapidly evolving

---

[22] As an example of the difficulty of collecting reliable data on partner forces, the Special Inspector General for Afghanistan Reconstruction indicated concern that, despite a well-resourced mission, "measures of [Afghan National Defense and Security Forces] capabilities and effectiveness have never been very reliable and are getting worse" (John F. Sopko, "Assessing the Capabilities and Effectiveness of the Afghan National Defense and Security Forces," testimony before the Subcommittee on Oversight and Investigations, Committee on Armed Services, U.S. House of Representatives, February 12, 2016). For example of the importance of subjective indicators, U.S. Government Accountability Office, *Security Assistance: Evaluations Needed to Determine Effectiveness of U.S. Aid to Lebanon's Security Forces*, Washington, D.C., GAO-13-289, March 19, 2013, p. 20.

[23] The quote is from Joint Publication (JP) 3-05, *Special Operations*, Washington, D.C.: Joint Chiefs of Staff, July 16, 2014, p. I-2. Another useful discussion is in Susan S. White, Rose A. Mueller-Hanson, David W. Dorsey, Elaine D. Pulakos, Michelle M. Wisecarver, Edwin A. Deagle III, and Kip G. Mendini, *Developing Adaptive Proficiency in Special Forces Officers*, Arlington, Va.: U.S. Army Research Institute for the Behavioral and Social Sciences, 2005. Improvisation is reportedly particularly important for Special Forces (SF) and civil affairs (CA) soldiers:

> [W]e earlier discussed a willingness to bend rules and improvise. But as we also noted, Rangers, because of the kind of work that they do, adhere strictly to the rules. SEALs,

environments in which they operate. This dynamism means that the "theory of change"—"how and why the commander believes the tasks that have been laid out will result in the desired end state"—can itself change rapidly.[24] Critical assessments are unlikely to be static.[25] Third, an added challenge when working in hostile or *denied environments* is that standard approaches for measuring population-centric effects (e.g., polling of local nationals using a locally contracted firm) may not be reliable.[26] Fourth, SOF operations are frequently designed to influence populations both physically and *cognitively* (with the ultimate goal of behavior change).[27] Measuring operational impacts in this cognitive

---

> too, follow standard operating procedures and tactics in their operations, for much the same reason Rangers do. Emphasis on improvisation is probably more characteristic of SF and is also a way of life for CA, in this case particularly because of a lack of resources and the restrictions that mark much of their work. (David Tucker and Christopher J. Lamb, *United States Special Operations Forces*, New York: Columbia University Press, 2007, p. 68)

[24] This definition is from Jan Osburg, Christopher Paul, Lisa Saum-Manning, Dan Madden, and Leslie Adrienne Payne, *Assessing Locally Focused Stability Operations*, Santa Monica, Calif.: RAND Corporation, RR-387-A, 2014, p. xiv. Osburg et al., 2014, p. xvi, indicates that the theory of changes allows "the assessment team to identify the appropriate inputs, outputs, and outcomes to measure and also enables it to determine whether critical assumptions built into the CONOP [concept of operations] may, if proven faulty, require the commander to adjust the campaign plan."

[25] ATP 5-0.3, 2015, p. ix, notes that "complex, ill structured, and adaptive operating environments [encountered in recent military operations] quickly overwhelmed existing assessment doctrine." Development professionals encounter a similar difficulty in complex settings because a theory of change "requires a commitment to take a reflective, critical and honest approach to answer difficult questions about how our efforts might influence change, given the political realities, uncertainties and complexities" (Isabel Vogel, *Review of the Use of 'Theory of Change' in International Development*, UK Department of International Development, April 2012, p. 5).

[26] As an example, every local national survey firm accused the others of fabricating surveys (filling out surveys in cafes, etc.), an accusation that is very difficult to validate using standard methods.

[27] As an example, the "Command Vision" of Special Operations Command Central (SOCCENT) commanded by then-MG Kenneth Tovo in 2013 was to

> *[s]hape the cognitive domain . . . SOCCENT will employ the full spectrum of SOF capability to affect individuals, organizations, and societies in the physical and cognitive realm in order to ensure that behaviors and attitudes are consistent with USG [U.S. government] interests.*

domain is particularly difficult because the goals are not always easy to translate into objective measures; the effects of these operations may only accrue over long periods; and there is frequently no shared understanding of the value proposition of these efforts.[28]

Our approach for addressing all four of these SOF-unique challenges relies on novel and creative uses of data, described in Chapter Four and illustrated in Chapter Five. The first is the utilization of all types of ambient data, which include individuals' digital fingerprints (e.g., social media and other digital communication), satellite-based imagery (e.g., movement, agricultural production), and traditional media (e.g., newspapers). Available technologies allow us to overcome the first, third, and fourth SOF-specific challenges by rapidly mining these data sets to generate systematic and objective measures of such otherwise-difficult-to-measure factors as enemy and partner-force morale, civilian pattern of life, and economic activity in denied areas. Systematic collection of operational data—e.g., SITREPs, intelligence reporting—provides an additional data source for capturing these difficult-to-measure effects and, importantly, provides an adaptive data source for describing the types of activities that SOF is conducting to achieve effects. Process tracing methods, discussed later in this report in greater detail, provide one means of ascertaining the effectiveness of SOF activities on partner efforts.

Research Approach

The assessment approach detailed in this report—which was designed to satisfy the requirements of an operational-level assessment, overcome

---

> Ideally, our partners are willing and able to maintain stability, our enemies are unable to disrupt civil society of our partners and allies, and the indigenous population pursues goals compatible with U.S. interests. (U.S. Special Operations Command, Fact Book 2013, Tampa, Fla., 2013, p. 24; emphasis added)

28 See Christopher Paul, Jessica Yeats, Colin P. Clarke, and Miriam Matthews, *Assessing and Evaluating Department of Defense Efforts to Inform, Influence, and Persuade: Desk Reference*, Santa Monica, Calif.: RAND Corporation, RR-809/1-OSD, 2015, for a discussion (especially Box 2.1 on p. 23, pp. 51–55, and pp. 73–104).

the myriad challenges assessments face, and be appropriate for SOF activities—relies on four types of research activities. The first of these activities, which was designed to provide an evidenced-based depiction of how SOF achieves effects, was a review of recent SOF efforts. In all, we reviewed a dozen SOF efforts that lasted longer than one year, which provided a broad understanding of how SOF operational-level commanders and their staffs combine special operations core activities to achieve effects in accordance with higher command guidance.

The second was a detailed review of the extensive literature on assessments, to capture best practices on how to overcome the challenges detailed earlier. This included a review of the assessment literature focused on military operations, with a focus on the efforts of analysts supporting the military and the interagency community through the past 15 years of war and of social scientists examining a broader range of programming in contexts similar to those in which SOF is likely to operate.

A third, which was designed to describe potential emerging assessment techniques that SOF might consider, was a series of consultations with assessment elements of private-sector enterprises involved in areas of the world and/or activities that overlap with SOF missions. We consulted with experienced individuals involved in assessment product development and advertising for emerging markets, conducting interventions to improve international development and health, mining and drilling in frontier environments, and exploiting big data and social media.

The final stage of this research was a deliberative and consultative process with representatives from across the SOF enterprise to validate the assessment approach emerging from the three previous activities. For this process, we developed a sample assessment using our methodology and available data for SOJTF Operation Inherent Resolve. We presented the methodology and results for structured feedback and critique by a diverse audience of SOF practitioners, including senior-level representatives from across the SOF enterprise and the theater special operations commands.[29] This process facilitated further revision and

[29] The theater special operations commands are subordinate commands of U.S. Special Operations Command.

refinement of the analytic process to improve clarity and applicability to real-world situations and the constraints of SOF operational environments.

Organization of This Report

Chapter Two establishes an understanding of the activities to be assessed by reviewing the various ways in which SOF achieves effects. This chapter draws on newly developed Army SOF (ARSOF) value propositions, doctrinal core activities, and typical lines of effort (LOEs) in contemporary SOF operational plans. This chapter also establishes the rationale for an LOE-based assessment approach for SOF. Chapter Three then develops standardized MOEs for each common SOF LOE and describes the types of data and indicators that can be used for tracking progress along the objectives for each of these LOEs. Chapter Four provides an intuitive step-by-step guide for developing and implementing a SOF operational-level assessment that is designed to be broadly applicable across the SOF enterprise. Chapter Five illustrates our proposed assessment process using the fictional example of conflict between Atropia and Ariana. Chapter Six outlines some final considerations for SOF that emerged from the development of this report. It discusses the enormous value that operational data (e.g., SITREPs) can have for supporting SOF assessments—provided that the data is consistently collected and appropriately structured. The chapter also explores the potential value of emerging technologies and data (e.g., social media) for SOF assessments. The chapter concludes with a discussion of how LOE-based assessments need to be modified to evaluate steady-state or preventive missions. A companion volume provides two appendixes, which present our assessment toolbox (Appendix A) and describe the criteria for MOE selection (Appendix B).[30]

---

[30] Linda Robinson, Daniel Egel, and Ryan Andrew Brown, *Measuring the Effectiveness of Special Operations: Appendixes*, Santa Monica, Calif.: RAND Corporation, RR-2504/1-A, 2019.

CHAPTER TWO

Line of Effort–Based Assessment Approach

LOE-based approaches are now common for strategic- and operational-level assessments of military operations. Military campaigns are typically divided into LOEs, each of which specifies an objective (and sometimes intermediate military objectives); these objectives provide the standard against which the assessment aims to measure progress. LOE-based assessment approaches then conduct separate "lines of analysis" for each LOE.[1] This provides our central organizing construct. Within each LOE, the assessment team must then identify specific activities and the effects they are designed to achieve, as well as the causal processes linking activities with effects. In developing the operational plan and LOEs, the planners should have framed the explicit theory of change that spells out how the activities to be undertaken will result in the achievement of desired effects and ultimately the stated objectives, as stipulated in in joint planning doctrine.[2] The assessment team should rely on the operational plan and its underlying theory of change as a starting point to map the plausible causal pathways and, in turn, develop appropriate MOEs to determine whether these effects are occurring.[3] An LOE-based assessment that is

---

[1] Alejandro S. Hernandez, Julian Ouellet, and Christopher J. Nannini, "Circular Logic and Constant Progress: IW Assessments in Afghanistan," in George W. Casey, Jr., Leo J. Blanken, Hy Rothstein, and Jason J. Lepore, eds., *Assessing War: The Challenge of Measuring Success and Failure*," Washington, D.C.: Georgetown University Press, 2015, p. 227.

[2] JP 3-05, 2014.

[3] Figure VI-14 in JP 5-0, *Joint Planning*, Washington, D.C.: Joint Chiefs of Staff, June 16, 2017, p. VI-30, outlines a generic logic model to help assessment teams trace the postulated

developed alongside the overall planning process, and nested within the overall plan, is a valuable resource for guiding an operational-level commander's decisionmaking.[4]

An LOE-based approach is particularly appropriate for SOF operational-level assessment. In fact, a core feature of LOEs in the development and execution of SOF operational-level efforts is that they "facilitate feedback and assessment in a way that effectively informs the reframing process and provides useful information."[5] Further, the complex nature of SOF efforts—which typically (1) include a combination of SOF's 12 core activities, as defined in joint doctrine;[6] (2) are conducted in challenging circumstances; and (3) achieve effects both directly through the agency of SOF and indirectly through partners, proxies, or populations—makes an LOE-based assessment approach attractive because aligning each SOF activity with a measurable outcome quickly becomes intractable.

In this chapter, we describe how these SOF LOEs can be used as a framework for guiding assessment. The first section focuses on describing how SOF delivers effects, describing both the recently developed *pillars of capability* and SOF core activities. The second section then characterizes the key SOF LOEs and describes the relationships between these LOEs, pillars of capability, and core activities. Together, these discussions lay the groundwork for the development of MOEs and evidence-based assessment methods described in the following chapters. Chapter Five will describe the complexities and challenges for integrating this LOE-based assessment approach into an overall campaign assessment.

---

causal pathways and the development of appropriate MOEs. See also Paul, Yeats, et al., 2015, Chapter Five.

[4] Hernandez, Ouellet, and Nannini, 2015, p. 228.

[5] Paruchabutr et al., 2014, p. C-8.

[6] Also, the "execution of one core activity may have operational or strategic impact on other core activities being planned or executed" (JP 3-05, 2014, p. x).

Pillars of Capability and SOF Core Activities

This section describes the nature of special operations according to recent command guidance, current doctrine, and special operations as they have recently been conducted. The purpose of this section is to fully describe how SOF delivers effects and the range of U.S. special operations capabilities and core activities and to broadly characterize how they are commonly employed in integrated and sustained efforts that frequently last for several years.

Clearly articulating what special operations are has proven especially challenging because of their varied nature and the nuances in how they aim to achieve effects. The complexity arises fundamentally from two features: (1) Special operations may achieve effects directly through the agency of SOF or indirectly through partners, proxies, or populations, and (2) they often achieve effects through combined application, such as the simultaneous use of CA operations (CAO), military information support operations (MISO), and partner-force operations.

This complexity is captured in the official U.S. military definition of *special operations*, which emphasizes the difficulty of the operations and the challenging circumstances under which they are conducted:

> Operations requiring unique modes of employment, tactical techniques, equipment and training often conducted in hostile, denied, or politically sensitive environments and characterized by one or more of the following: time sensitive, clandestine, low visibility, conducted with and/or through indigenous forces, requiring regional expertise, and/or a high degree of risk.[7]

To provide the fullest possible exposition of special operations briefly, we first summarize the value propositions USASOC has developed, which provide a useful broad characterization of how varied SOF activities can deliver effects in various ways. Then, we summarize the current doctrinal core activities that are combinations of the constituent activities and the core mission set that SOF typically performs. In

---

[7] JP 3-05, 2014, p. ix.

the following section, we will describe how these value propositions and core activities nest into a prototypical integrated special operations plan, which typically includes multiple core activities organized into LOEs.

SOF Value Propositions

USASOC developed four *pillars of capability*, or value propositions, to provide external audiences a readily understood description of "what SOF does." This description does not replace doctrine but serves as a more synthesized summary of the basic value that SOF provides as part of the armed forces and the U.S. government. These four pillars of capability, described in Table 2.1 based on the USASOC-developed definitions,[8] "are employed throughout the operational spectrum and across all campaign phases, including interagency or coalition-led campaigns and operations."[9]

The first of these four pillars—the "indigenous approach"—achieves effects exclusively through partnerships with indigenous forces, which may exist prior to SOF engagement or may be recruited from civilian populations. SOF may perform a restricted or wide set of activities alongside the partner (e.g., conduct combat operations, provide advice and enablers, or merely train and equip the partner), but the indigenous approach explicitly excludes unilateral operations. For the other three pillars—precision targeting, understanding and influence, and crisis response—effects can be achieved unilaterally or by partners, with SOF either enabling the partners or not. These distinctions matter for assessments, as will be discussed further in the next section and then in more detail in Chapter Three.

---

[8] USASOC, *Communicating the ARSOF Narrative and Setting the Course to 2035*, Fort Bragg, Calif.: John F. Kennedy Special Warfare Center and School, 2017a, p. 4-5.

[9] Scott R. Gourley, "The Four Pillars of Army SOF: Lt. Gen. Ken Tovo Describes USASOC Today," interview, *The Year in Special Operations 2017–2018*, 2017, p. 51.

Table 2.1
Four Pillars of SOF Capability

Pillar	Definition
Indigenous approach	"[A] means to address challenges to regional stability with and through populations and partner forces empowered by persistent ARSOF engagement. Through the approach, ARSOF leverage nascent capability within population, transforming indigenous mass into combat power. Since World War II, ARSOF elements have amassed unique institutional and operational expertise in living among, training, advising, and fighting alongside people of foreign culture, achieve effects with and through partner forces."
Precision targeting	"[D]irect action and counter-network activities . . . employed against uniquely difficult target sets that may require operating in uncertain or hostile environments, careful and focused application of force, and significant intelligence and operational preparation. . . . They create precise physical and psychological effects and can be used to collapse threat networks through deliberate targeting of critical nodes, as demonstrated in counterterrorism campaigns."
Understanding and influence	"The SOF network of personnel, assets, and international partnerships represent means by which to obtain early understanding of trends, emerging local, regional, and transregional threats, and where opportunities exist for advancing U.S. objectives. Employment of the SOF network provides capabilities needed to influence outcomes in all campaign phases and especially in environments experiencing conflict short of overt war."
Crisis response	"[P]rovides national decision makers with agile, tailorable, and rapidly employable special operations formations necessary to respond to emergencies. These forces provide options to rescue people under threat, to recover sensitive materials such as WMD components, or to address other short notice requirements."

SOURCE: Definitions are from USASOC, 2017a, p. 4-5.

SOF Core Activities in Doctrine

As defined in joint doctrine, SOF capabilities are employed in 12 "core activities."[10] These core activities, which are enumerated in Table 2.2, are extremely heterogeneous. The list includes activities as diverse as direct action, which achieves clearly identifiable physical effects, and CAO, which range from assessing populations and environments to

[10] SOF activities are also defined in U.S. Code (U.S. Code Title 10, §167, Unified Combatant Command for Special Operations Forces, as of January 3, 2012); this list of activities differs slightly from that in current joint doctrine. We have relied on joint doctrine as the most recent official publication and that used most often in operational planning.

Table 2.2
Doctrinal SOF Core Activities

Core Activity	Abbreviation	Description
Direct action	DA	Short-duration strikes and other small-scale offensive actions conducted as special operations in hostile, denied, or diplomatically sensitive environments employing specialized military capabilities to seize, destroy, capture, exploit, recover, or damage designated targets.
Special reconnaissance	SR	Reconnaissance and surveillance actions conducted as special operations in hostile, denied, or diplomatically and/or politically sensitive environments to collect or verify information of strategic or operational significance, employing military capabilities not normally found in conventional forces.
Counter–weapons of mass destruction	CWMD	Efforts against actors of concern to curtail the conceptualization, development, possession, proliferation, use, and effects of WMD, related expertise, materials, technologies, and means of delivery.
Counterterrorism	CT	Activities and operations taken to neutralize terrorists and their organizations and networks to render them incapable of using violence to instill fear and coerce governments or societies to achieve terrorist goals.
Unconventional warfare	UW	Activities conducted to enable a resistance movement or insurgency to coerce, disrupt, or overthrow a government or occupying power by operating through or with an underground, auxiliary, and guerrilla force in a denied area.
Foreign internal defense	FID	Participation by civilian and military agencies of a government in any of the action programs taken by another government or other designated organization to free and protect its society from subversion, lawlessness, insurgency, terrorism, and other threats to its security.
Security force assistance	SFA	Department of Defense activities that support the development of the capacity and capability of foreign security forces and their supporting institutions.
Hostage rescue and recovery	HR	A personnel recovery method used to recover isolated personnel who have been specifically designated as hostages.

Table 2.2—Continued

Core Activity	Abbreviation	Description
Counterinsurgency	COIN	Comprehensive civilian and military efforts designed to simultaneously defeat and contain insurgency and address its root causes.
Foreign humanitarian assistance	HA	Department of Defense activities conducted outside the United States and its territories to directly relieve or reduce human suffering, disease, hunger, or privation.
Military information support operations	MISO	Planned operations to convey selected information and indicators to foreign audiences to influence their emotions, motives, objective reasoning, and ultimately the behavior of foreign governments, organizations, groups, and individuals in a manner favorable to the originator's objectives.
Civil affairs operations	CA	Actions planned, coordinated executed, and assessed to enhance awareness of, and manage the interaction with, the civil component of the operational environment; identify and mitigate underlying causes of instability within civil society; and/or or involve the application of functional specialty skills normally the responsibility of civil government.

SOURCES: JP 3-05, 2014; definitions quoted from JP 1-02, *DoD Dictionary of Military and Associated Terms*, August 2018.

treating causes of instability to enabling civil government functions. Some activities are discrete actions (e.g., special reconnaissance), while others are multifaceted operations with potentially strategic impact (e.g., countering weapons of mass destruction [WMD]). Counterinsurgency (COIN), foreign internal defense, and unconventional warfare are typically conceived of as entire campaigns in themselves.

Typical Special Operations Forces Lines of Effort

SOF operational-level plans are typically parsed into LOEs, which link SOF activities to the objectives of the plan.[11] In this section we characterize four typical LOEs of SOF operational-level headquarters and their objectives based on a review of recent long-duration SOF efforts,[12] and describe their linkages to the core activities and pillars of capability just described. As described later, LOEs are aligned with the strategic objectives that SOF aims to achieve, and they are executed through SOF core activities and capabilities.

Table 2.3 summarizes the relationships between these LOEs and their objectives and the value propositions and core activities. This schematic representation does not include all the contributions of core activities: For example, in addition to influencing the population by addressing factors of instability and governance, CAO include area assessments that provide understanding and secure access and placement for other SOF activities to occur. Similarly, the influence LOE is executed in specific ways through psychological operations (PSYOP) and CA but also through the wider activities of SOF, which have an effect on the sentiments and behaviors of populations, friendly forces, and adversaries. MOEs may be developed specifically for other forms of influence.

On occasion, intelligence and understanding may be treated as separate LOEs in some SOF plans, particularly if they are outputs to be provided to higher headquarters or other forces or for a steady-state campaign rather than contingency or combat operations. In these former cases (for example, a theater special operations command plan), MOEs can be developed to assess intelligence or understanding LOEs. In this report, we consider intelligence and understanding (including

---

[11] Paruchabutr et al., 2014, p. VI-6. The SOF operational plan is generally nested under an overarching operational plan of the joint force command, if there is one, and the geographic combatant command's campaign plan. This document uses "SOF campaign," where appropriate, to connote the integrated effects that SOF aim to achieve through the combined application of their own capabilities.

[12] Our review included SOF plans for campaigns conducted in Afghanistan, Iraq, Syria, Pakistan, Philippines, East and Northwest Africa, Central Africa, Yemen, and Colombia.

Table 2.3
Lines of Effort, Objectives, Value Propositions, and SOF Core Activities

LOE	Objectives	Value Propositions	Core Activities
Develop, enable, and employ partner force	Acquire independent and capable partner	Indigenous approach	Foreign internal defense Unconventional warfare Security force assistance COIN
Precision targeting	Degrade or suppress enemy	Precision targeting	Direct action Counterterrorism Special reconnaissance
Influence via MISO	Decrease support for enemy Increase support for partner	Understanding and influence	MISO
Influence via CAO	Population denies support to the enemy Population supports partner	Understanding and influence	CAO

NOTE: Based on review of unpublished SOF campaigns.

preparation of the environment activities) as preparatory and ongoing activities that enable all LOEs. From this perspective, they are inputs to the LOEs that produce the overall campaign effects.

Develop, Enable, and Employ Partner Forces

Building and employing a *capable partner* that is willing to support U.S. military objectives is a core component of SOF efforts. This LOE—which involves the recruitment, training, equipping, advising, and sustainment of partner forces—has been a key element in SOF long-duration efforts against both state and nonstate actors.[13] In some

---

[13] Linda Robinson, Patrick B. Johnston, and Gillian S. Oak, *U.S. Special Operations Forces in the Philippines, 2001–2014*, Santa Monica, Calif.: RAND Corporation, RR-1236-OSD, 2016; David P. Fridovich and Fred T. Krawchuk, "Winning in the Pacific, The Special Operations Forces Indirect Approach," *Joint Force Quarterly*, No. 44, 1st Quarter 2007,

cases, these partner forces are mobilized for short-term purposes and demobilized (or channeled into other armed forces) after short-term goals have been met; in other cases, the goal is to build self-sustaining forces that can persist after SOF withdraws. While building partner forces is not unique to SOF,[14] U.S. SOF has a long history of establishing, training, and advising a wide variety of partner forces across the globe, including Iraq, Colombia, Afghanistan, and the Philippines,[15] where U.S. SOF has recruited, trained, equipped, advised, and helped sustain partner forces.

This LOE, in particular, requires careful parsing to determine all the component activities and the effects to be assessed. Partner development can include a range of recruitment, selection, training, and initial equipping, as well as construction of institutions for force generation, sustainment, education and higher-echelon headquarters, if the objective is to assist a partner force in obtaining permanent independent operating capability. Employment can range from unilateral operations to operations assisted in a variety of ways with advice, intelligence, various support functions, and combat advising at all echelons under various rules of engagement. Assessments will generally want to evaluate two facets: the effectiveness of the partner itself (which can be due to many variables) and the effectiveness of the various types of support that SOF is providing. The latter are the critical variables that the SOF command can most easily adjust; the intrinsic or innate partner-force factors (as well as outside influences on the partner) may not be amenable to change. Similarly, other outside influences on the partner force may be beyond the ability of SOF to alter.

As described previously, the indigenous approach is, by definition, conducted with other partner forces—which may exist prior to

---

p. 27; Headquarters, Combined Joint Special Operations Task Force–Afghanistan, *Village Stability Operations and Afghan Local Police: Bottom-Up Counterinsurgency*, 2011.

[14] Austin Long, Stephanie Pezard, Bryce Loidolt, and Todd C. Helmus, *Locals Rule: Historical Lessons for Creating Local Defense Forces for Afghanistan and Beyond*, Santa Monica, Calif.: RAND Corporation, MG-1232-CFSOCC-A, 2012.

[15] Robinson, Johnston, and Oak 2016; Fridovich and Krawchuk, 2007; USASOC, 2016; Headquarters, Combined Joint Special Operations Task Force–Afghanistan, 2011.

SOF engagement or may be recruited from civilian populations—but not unilaterally. The other three pillars (precision targeting, understanding and influence, and crisis response) may be unilateral, enabled by partners, or wholly partnered activities, depending on the circumstances. These distinctions matter for the purpose of assessments, as we will explain later.

Precision Targeting

The use of precision targeting to *degrade or suppress enemy forces* is a second core SOF LOE. This includes both direct-action activities—i.e., "short-duration strikes and other small-scale offensive actions . . . in hostile, denied, or diplomatically and/or politically sensitive environments"—and counternetwork activities focused on understanding and neutralizing threat networks.[16] Precision targeting includes *unilateral direct action*, in which U.S. SOF, potentially partnered with conventional units, conduct direct-action missions; *combined U.S.-indigenous direct action*, in which U.S. SOF partners with indigenous elements; and *kinetic strikes*, which rely on precision-guided munitions to attack targets. These operations achieve effects both directly and indirectly. The direct effects include the destruction of a specific threat (e.g., an individual, a key piece of materiel) or the degradation of threat networks through "deliberate targeting of critical enemy nodes."[17] Indirect effects include the creation of time and space for operations by SOF, indigenous, or other elements and the inherent psychological influence these operations have on the cost calculus of adversaries and potential adversaries.[18]

---

[16] The definition of *direct action* is from JP 3-05, 2014, p. x. The heuristic definition of *counternetwork activities* is from Joint Warfighting Center, *Commander's Handbook for Attack the Network*, Vers. 1.0, Suffolk, Va.: Joint Doctrine Support Division, 2011.

[17] Gourley, 2017.

[18] Gourley, 2017.

Influence via Military Information Support Operations

MISO are carried out by PSYOP units staffed with personnel trained in this military occupational specialty.[19] As noted earlier, SOF seeks to achieve many of their objectives through influence, and this influence can be exercised in a wide variety of ways. SOF doctrine, education, and training emphasize the importance of the human dimension and cultural awareness so that special operators may build relationships with their partner forces, the population, the host-nation government and the interagency and coalition partners they work alongside. MISO and CAO are selected for specific MOE development and assessment in the influence LOEs because their activities seek to achieve effects primarily through influence pathways.

MISO are designed to "convey selected information and indicators to foreign audiences to influence their emotions, motives, objective reasoning, and ultimately the behavior of foreign governments, organizations, groups, and individuals."[20] MISO use a wide variety of media and communication platforms—from the more traditional leaflets, loudspeakers, and radio stations to the internet via social media and other means. Joint doctrine emphasizes that MISO are activities explicitly aimed at influencing behavior to distinguish them from other activities that may incidentally influence behavior.[21]

---

[19] We use *influence* as the LOE because that is the current usage in the special operations community. Some SOF plans have previously used *information operations* as a line of operations, but this is a broader doctrinal term comprising numerous information-related activities. SOF may make use of tactical military deception, which is a distinct information operation. MISO are a SOF core activity that has also been described as PSYOP (until 2011). As part of an ongoing effort to reinstate the term *PSYOP*, which is still used by other allied militaries, USASOC issued guidance in 2017 that changed official terminology for its units from *MISO* back to *PSYOP*. See USASOC, "Designation of Psychological Operations Units Assigned to the United States Army Special Operations Command," memorandum for the record, October 27, 2017b. However, current doctrine still uses the term *MISO* to describe the activities that PSYOP units conduct.

[20] JP 3-05, 2014; Curtis Boyd, "The Future of MISO," *Special Warfare*, Vol. 24, No. 1, January–February 2011.

[21] JP 3-13.2, *Military Information Support Operations*, Washington, D.C.: Joint Chiefs of Staff, December 20, 2011, pp. I-2, 3. The most recent public Army doctrine is Field Manual (FM) 3-53, *Military Information Support Operations*, Washington, D.C.: Headquarters, U.S. Army, 2013.

Influence via Civil Affairs Operations

CAO are actions planned, executed, and assessed by CA forces to enhance awareness of and manage interactions with the civil component of the operational environment, identify and mitigate underlying causes of instability within civil society, or involve the application of functional specialty skills normally the responsibility of civil government. These operations all achieve effects that fall under the influence LOE. Through interaction with the existing civil component of the operational environment, CA forces directly influence both government and populations. Their operations to address causes of instability influence both governments and populations and seek to reduce the attraction of enemy forces and their room for maneuver. When the government is weak or nonexistent, CAO may support the organization of government or the temporary exercise of some of its functions. The 95th CA Brigade has begun to develop an overarching conceptual framework to represent the objectives and effects that SOF-focused CA forces specifically aim to achieve.[22] The governance and countergovernance rubric is intended to squarely focus on the objectives of gaining population support for a legitimate governing entity while denying the enemy's bid to achieve control over the population. This rubric aims to reduce the potential confusion of tactical activities that CA conducts with the overarching objectives it seeks to achieve as part of the SOF plan.

Summary

As noted earlier, this schematic representation of SOF LOEs for typical SOF plans does not encompass every possible LOE, but these are common elements of long-duration efforts. The crisis response pillar is understood to be an enduring requirement that SOF must be prepared to execute on short notice, but crisis response is not an LOE that is continuously executed as part of an integrated SOF plan. Together,

[22] Jason Slider, "95th Civil Affairs Brigade Capabilities," slide, Fort Bragg, N.C.: U.S. Army Special Operations Command, 2017.

the four LOEs represent a valid schematic approach to the way special operations capabilities are applied, taking into account these caveats.

In the following three chapters, we illustrate how SOF assessment can proceed from an LOE-based starting point. In Chapter Three, we begin by identifying the broad, generic objectives of each LOE and provide starting points for MOEs that logically flow from these objectives. Of course, the assessment process itself requires a detailed and careful grounding of objectives and MOEs in the context of specific operations. We provide a seven-step assessment process in Chapter Four, then use a worked example in Chapter Five to illustrate how this process would work in the context of specific activities and desired effects.

CHAPTER THREE

Measures of Effectiveness for SOF Assessment

Current joint doctrine defines assessment as

> a continuous activity that supports decision making by ascertaining progress toward accomplishing a task, creating an effect, achieving an objective, or attaining an end state for the purpose of developing, adapting, and refining plans and for making campaigns and operations more effective.[1]

In the context of assessing a campaign or operational-level plan, MOEs are used to assess changes in system behavior, capability, or operational environment that are tied to measuring the attainment of an end state, achievement of an objective, or creation of an effect. In the context of operational assessment, an *indicator* is a specific piece of information that indicates the condition, state, or existence of something and provides a reliable means to ascertain performance or effectiveness.[2] When properly designed, MOEs "provide a framework for conducting trend analysis of system behavior or capability changes that occur over time, based on the observation of specific, discrete indicators."[3] This implies a cyclical assessment process based on ongoing data collection and analysis.

---

1 JP 5-0, Ch. VI, Operation Assessment, p. VI-1.

2 JP 5-0, p. VI-24, states further that "indicators should be relevant, observable or collectable, responsive, and resourced."

3 Joint Staff, 2011, p. x.

MOEs are typically developed in a four-phase process.[4] The first phase is the identification of intended effects associated with the objectives of each LOE. The second is a brainstorming session that considers a wide variety of possible MOEs. In the third phase, the MOEs are evaluated for inclusion based on their *relevance* (i.e., a direct link with the activities of that LOE), *measurability* (i.e., can be measured with available data), *malleability* (i.e., are reasonably expected to change within the time frame of analysis), and *distinctness* (i.e., they are mutually exclusive).[5] The fourth phase is identifying data that can be used for measuring change in that MOE and the selection of appropriate indicators for tracking progress.

In this chapter, we develop a set of baseline MOEs for each LOE (and associated objectives) described in Chapter Two and then describe and justify each MOE following the criteria just outlined.[6] We also identify three commonly available types of data sources that might be used to develop indicators for specific MOEs, as well as specific indicators. *Operational data* include data, such as SITREPs and intelligence reporting collected and created by military units (and other interagency elements supporting these units) as part of their operations. These data provide geographically and temporally precise information on unit activities, the operational environment, and how both are evolving. *Ambient data* include a wide variety of data—social media, satellite imagery, news, etc.—that are typically produced and collected by other entities where military operations are being conducted.

---

[4] This is a simplified version of the eight-step method offered in the *Commander's Handbook for Assessment Planning and Execution* (Joint Staff, 2011). Specifically, we have consolidated the development and evaluation of MOE indicators (Step 4 and Step 5, respectively) into a single step, have omitted additional steps for validating the selection of MOEs (Step 6 and Step 7), and have excluded the weighting of MOEs (Step 8), given that the number of MOEs is deliberately parsimonious. (Joint Staff, 2011, pp. III-9–II-13).

[5] These criteria are based on JDN 1-15, 2015, pp. II-8 and A-6. See Appendix B for additional detail and explanation.

[6] Our discussion does not focus on crisis response because this usually involves a discrete activity with a binary outcome, e.g., securing WMD or hostages. While preparations for crisis response may need to be assessed by some commands, and degrees of readiness may lend themselves to measures of performance (MOPs); assessing the effectiveness of actual crisis response operations may be fairly straightforward as their outcomes tend to be binary.

Assessment-specific data include polling or survey data based on structured data collection instruments (in which individuals select from a list of precoded responses to a series of questions) and interviews or focus groups (which elicit less-structured data).[7] This category of data is more labor intensive and expensive to generate, so it is ideally combined with the other, existing forms of data. The data discussions in the step-by-step assessment process in the Chapter Four and in Appendix A provide additional details on the specifics of the different data types and the considerations for employing each.[8]

Chapter Four describes the process for using these MOEs to prepare for and implement an operational-level assessment of SOF. The step-by-step process outlined in Chapter Four also describes the role of MOPs in a SOF operational-level assessment by providing an intermediary in the assessment process by tracking whether the tactical elements are performing effectively. MOPs thus assess whether the subordinate forces are "doing things right," while MOEs assess whether the operational-level headquarters is "doing the right things," which is the goal of an operational-level assessment.[9] Chapter Five provides a worked example using these foundational MOEs, so that the reader can see how the generic MOEs in this chapter could be applied in a specific operational setting.

We emphasize that the MOEs presented here are only some of those that might be developed; these could be considered basic, foundational MOEs that meet the standards put forth earlier and address common LOEs. It is important for the assessment team to consider additional possible MOEs that may meet standards and shed additional light on LOEs, particularly those that are more nuanced in execution or objective.

---

[7] For example, IST Research conducts polling via mobile phones, having advertised for participation via a Facebook page. See Renuka Hermon, "Addressing Human Security Issues: Cause Award Honoree IST Research," June 16, 2017, for more information on IST Research.

[8] Appendix A is in the companion volume: Robinson, Egel, and Brown, 2019.

[9] Deployable Training Division, 2013.

Develop, Enable, and Employ Partner Force

The develop, enable, and employ partner force LOE has two major objectives: (1) SOF builds and sustains the partner force, and (2) the partner force degrades the enemy. This section describes the MOEs and associated indicators required to assess these two primary objectives, as summarized in Table 3.1. In this section, we describe each proposed MOE and indicators that can be used to assess that MOE.

Partner-Force Strength and Sustainability

Partner-force *strength* assesses the status of the partner force (manpower, equipment, etc.) at a specific time, while *sustainability* is a measure of the partner force's ability to maintain its strength over time.[10] This MOE is directly and logically linked with the *develop* and *enable* components of the develop, enable, and employ partner force LOE.

Indicators for partner-force strength and sustainability include standard operational data usually collected by tactical units and headquarters—such as manpower (including recruitment, retention, and attrition), training institutions and levels of training, and equipment status and maintenance. Interviews with trainers and enablers (assessment data) can also provide indicators of partner-force strength and sustainability. For more-enduring missions, measures of sustainability should assess the partner force's ability to sustain itself, independent of SOF support.

---

[10] See Linda Robinson, *Assessment of the Politico-Military Campaign to Counter ISIL and Options for Adaptation*, Santa Monica, Calif.: RAND Corporation, RR-1290-OSD, 2016, pp. 37–41, for examples of partner-force strength and equipment assessment. For additional examples of frameworks to assess partner-force capacity, see Jefferson P. Marquis, Michael J. McNerney, S. Rebecca Zimmerman, Merrie Archer, Jeremy Boback, and Dave Stebbins, *Developing an Assessment, Monitoring, and Evaluation Framework for U.S. Department of Defense Security Cooperation*, Santa Monica, Calif.: RAND Corporation, RR-1611-OSD, 2016, and Christopher Paul, Brian J. Gordon, Jennifer D. P. Moroney, Lisa Saum-Manning, Beth Grill, Colin P. Clarke, and Heather Peterson, *A Building Partner Capacity Assessment Framework: Tracking Inputs, Outputs, Outcomes, Disrupters, and Workarounds*, Santa Monica, Calif.: RAND Corporation, RR-935-OSD, 2015.

Table 3.1
Measures of Effectiveness for Develop, Enable, and Employ Partner Force

		Indicators		
Objective	**MOE**	**Operational**	**Ambient**	**Assessment**
1. SOF builds and sustains the partner force	Partner-force strength and sustainability	**Mission tracker:** Force strength, attrition and recruitment, equipment		**Interviews:** Trainer and enabler perceptions of partner-force sustainability
	Partner-force operational capabilities	**SITREPS, mission tracker:** Operational tempo, range of missions, battlefield competence (command and control, etc.)		**Interviews:** Trainer and enabler perceptions of partner-force performance
	Partner-force morale and professionalism	**SITREPS:** Reports of partner-force corruption and abuse, voluntary recruitment rates, operational tempo despite casualties	**Social and traditional media:** Reports on the conduct of partner forces	**Interviews:** Trainer and enabler perceptions of partner-force morale and professionalism
2. Partner force degrades the enemy	Enemy territorial loss	**SITREPs, intelligence, intelligence, surveillance, and reconnaissance (ISR):** Changes in territory controlled by enemy	**Social and traditional media:** Reports, discussions of liberation and movement of forces	
	Disruption of enemy operations	**Intelligence:** Changes in enemy plans, tactics, or morale and will to fight		
	Enemy personnel and materiel losses	**SITREPs, intelligence:** Equipment and facilities destroyed, enemy attrition and desertion	**Social and traditional media:** Reports of loss of morale, battlefield damage	

Partner-Force Operational Capabilities

This MOE assesses partner-force battlefield capabilities and is directly connected to the *employ* component of the develop, enable, and employ partner force LOE.[11] As partner forces receive more training and experience under SOF guidance, the range, pace, and competence of partner operations can be expected to increase.[12] Thus, this MOE is sufficiently malleable at the pace of SOF operations.

Mission tracker data will contain information on the operational tempo and range of mission types partner forces engage in, and SITREPs will contain information on battlefield wins and losses and on partner-force performance. If necessary, interviews with trainers and enablers can provide further insights on partner-force performance and capabilities.

Standards for partner forces need to be objective and rigorous but should also take into account local culture, customs, and traditions to develop a realistic baseline from which progress can be measured.

Partner-Force Morale and Professionalism

When SOF is training a sustainable, long-term partner force, assessing morale and professionalism is especially critical to mission success. Even when SOF develops a partner for more-temporary purposes—i.e., not as part of an enduring security force of a partner nation—as in surrogate-force programs, the partner force's morale and professionalism will be important factors both for achieving results and for force protection considerations. SITREPs from tactical units can provide observations of both partner-force morale and ethical behavior or other aspects of professionalism. Voluntary recruitment rates and operational tempo in the face of casualties may also be useful indicators. Traditional and social media reports either praising or criticizing the conduct and behavior of partner forces can also be a valuable source of

---

[11] See Robinson, 2016, pp. 37–41, for a framework for and an assessment example of partner-force capabilities and operational breadth. For additional details on frameworks for assessing partner-force operational capabilities, see FM 3-07.1, *Security Force Assistance*, Washington, D.C., Headquarters, Department of the Army, May 2009, pp. 3:11–3:13.

[12] Joseph H. Felter, *Taking Guns to a Knife Fight: Effective Military Support to COIN*, Carlisle, Pa.: U.S. Army War College, 2008.

information. Meanwhile, interviews with trainers and enablers working with partner forces can reveal additional detail.

Enemy Territorial Loss

Where partner forces are actively engaging the enemy, this MOE provides a measure of enemy losses of territorial control linked with partner-force operations (whether independent or supported by SOF). In theaters with a high degree of kinetic activity, enemy territorial control can be expected to change at the pace of SOF operations. If partner forces are doing a significant amount of the fighting, enemy territorial loss can logically be attributed to the impact of these partner forces.[13] As a cautionary note, friendly and enemy lines are permeable in modern warfare because the enemy can stay embedded and hidden within the population for long periods. Thus, estimating territorial control can involve some guesswork and may require assigning degrees of enemy versus friendly control to specific areas.

Operational data streams, including SITREPs and intelligence, can include reports of changes in enemy territorial control. Additionally, in populations with significant social media and traditional media penetration, citizens and reporters may post images and text reports of the liberation of specific areas or enemy (and friendly) force movements.

Disruption of Enemy Operations

If partner forces are effectively employed in fighting the enemy, the risk of engagement with partner forces or the knowledge of partner-force effectiveness is presumed to eventually lead to enemy frustration and adjustments in enemy operations to avoid or counteract these effects. Thus, a disruption or change in enemy tactics and operations is logi-

---

13 See Seth G. Jones, Andrew Liepman, and Nathan Chandler, *Counterterrorism and Counterinsurgency in Somalia: Assessing the Campaign Against al Shabaab*, Santa Monica, Calif.: RAND Corporation, RR-1539-OSD, 2016, for an extensive discussion of insurgent territorial loss in the fight against Al-Shabaab. For a discussion of territorial change in the counter-ISIL campaign, see Robinson, 2016, p. 48. Clionadh Raleigh and Caitriona Dowd, "Armed Conflict Location and Event Data Project (ACLED) Codebook," Armed Conflict Location and Event Data Project website, 2015, pp. 8–10, provides a useful taxonomy of different types of events resulting in territorial loss and gain.

cally connected with partner-force effectiveness. Because most of this information will come from intelligence reporting, this MOE requires sufficient placement of intelligence assets in areas of interest.[14]

Insights from existing intelligence products (e.g., human intelligence (HUMINT), signals intelligence [SIGINT]) into enemy plans, desertion, recruitment, morale, or will to fight can provide an indicator for this MOE from operational data. Gathering information on enemy communications and tactics, techniques, and procedures is a routine aspect of intelligence collection, so assessment teams must only find ways of harvesting this information at sufficient fidelity and frequency to feed the assessment process.

Enemy Losses of Personnel and Materiel

This is perhaps the most direct and easily justifiable MOE for partner-force effectiveness when these partner forces are actively engaging the enemy. It makes an especially powerful case for the effectiveness of this LOE when partner forces are not only strong and sustainable (MOE 1) but are also able to impose considerable damage on the enemy force over time. Enemy attrition and destruction of enemy equipment or infrastructure should never be used in isolation, because this fails to account for the enemy's ability to replace losses through recruitment or manpower and material support from its partners.[15] Additionally, enemy losses through desertion, defection, loss of the will to fight, or other forms of attrition and capability depletion should be considered as part of the equation of enemy loss.

Much of the data to feed indicators of enemy attrition and enemy equipment and infrastructure losses will come from battle damage

---

[14] Jones, Liepman, and Chandler, 2016, provides an example in which Al-Shabaab's operational focus on targets outside Somalia provided evidence of its reduced in-country capabilities. Robinson, Johnston, and Oak, 2016, provides a more traditional case, in which SOF activities led to a decrease in enemy attacks over time.

[15] Many sources provide useful caveats and cautions against the sole use of enemy losses as an MOE (e.g., Connable, 2012). Also see John E. Mueller, "The Search for the 'Breaking Point' in Vietnam: The Statistics of a Deadly Quarrel," *International Studies Quarterly*, Vol. 24, No. 4, December 1980.

assessments,[16] SITREPs, and operational after-action reports. Intelligence reporting can also provide information on enemy desertion and other more subtle or harder to detect impact on the enemy. As with MOE 3, areas with functioning traditional media or social media penetration may yield ambient data on enemy losses through images and text reporting of battlefield effects.

Other Possible Measures of Effectiveness

We did not include measures of the degree to which partner forces protect the local population, enable freedom of movement, or open up opportunities for economic and other activity. These activities may be assessed, and MOEs can be developed to do so. However, these goals may be part of a wider security mission in which SOF and SOF-enabled forces are not the primary actors. When the SOF-enabled partner force is expected to provide this level of security, polling and interviews with local nationals can provide insights into perceptions of security, while satellite imagery can provide evidence of changes in migration, market activity, and other markers of economic change, as we will discuss later.

Precision Targeting

Precision targeting consists of "direct action and counter-network activities enabled by SOF unique intelligence, technology, and targeting processes."[17] *Direct action* includes "short-duration strikes and other small-scale offensive actions . . . in hostile, denied, or diplomatically and/or politically sensitive environments," and *counternetwork activities* focus on understanding and neutralizing threat networks.[18] Precision targeting includes *unilateral direct action*, in which U.S. SOF, potentially partnered with conventional units, conducts direct-action

---

[16] U.S. Joint Forces Command, *Commander's Handbook for Joint Battle Damage Assessment*, Joint Warfighting Center, June 1, 2004.

[17] Gourley, 2017.

[18] The definition of *direct action* is from JP 3-05, 2014, p. x. The heuristic definition of *counternetwork activities* is from Joint Warfighting Center, 2011.

missions; *combined U.S.-indigenous direct action*, in which U.S. SOF partner with indigenous elements; and *kinetic strikes*, which rely on precision-guided munitions to action targets.

Precision targeting has two primary objectives: (1) to reduce enemy capabilities and (2) to reduce population support for the enemy.[19] Objective 1 is quite similar to Objective 2 for the develop, enable, and employ partner force LOE and, therefore, shares the same MOEs and indicators (see Table 3.2). Just as partner-force operations are expected to force the enemy to change plans and tactics and produce enemy losses, precision strikes will have similar effects. These MOEs are therefore covered earlier, in the discussion of partner forces, and will not be repeated here. During the assessment process itself, it is important to specify whether effects in a particular area (or linked with a specific unit) are due to partner-force effects alone, precision targeting alone, or a combination of the two.

Objective 2 for this LOE is achieved in less directly, through demonstration of force as well as evidence of enemy losses and the cognitive and behavioral impact of these phenomena on the population.

MOEs for Objective 2

Reduced Population Expressions of Enemy Support

The ideal impact of precision targeting involves population recognition of SOF (and associated partner-force) capabilities, as well as a sense that the enemy has a tenuous hold and can be eliminated at any time.[20] A rational response to this realization is to decrease support for the dwindling and vulnerable enemy. A cautionary note here is that tar-

---

[19] See Robinson, 2016, for a discussion of the impact of precision targeting in the counter-ISIL campaign. Also see Patrick B. Johnston and Anoop K. Sarbahi, "The Impact of US Drone Strikes on Terrorism in Pakistan," *International Studies Quarterly*, Vol. 60, No. 2, June 2016, for evidence of the impact of precision strikes on enemy effectiveness.

[20] See Brendan Greenley and Dave Ohls, "Countering Radicalization: An Agent-Based Model of Precision Strike Campaigns," paper, April 6, 2014, for a theoretical and simulation-based treatment of this effect and of the role of collateral damage in decreasing precision strike effectiveness.

Table 3.2
Measures of Effectiveness for Precision Targeting

Objective	MOE	Indicators: Operational	Indicators: Ambient	Indicators: Assessment
1. Reduce enemy capabilities	*Disruptions of enemy operations*	***Intelligence:*** *Changes in enemy plans, tactics, or morale and will to fight*		
	Enemy personnel and materiel losses	***SITREPs, intelligence:*** *Equipment and facilities destroyed; enemy attrition and desertion*	***Social and traditional media:*** *Reports of loss of morale, battlefield damage*	
2. Reduce population support for the enemy	Reduced population expressions of enemy support		**Social and traditional media:** Celebrations of enemy defeat and destruction	**Polling:** Endorsement of negative statements about enemy **Interviews:** Antienemy themes
	Reduced materiel and other (e.g., intelligence, safe harbor, recruits) support to enemy from population	**Intelligence:** Enemy reports of reduction in recruitment, materiel, and other support from population **SITREPs:** Observations of less population collusion with enemy		

NOTE: Text in italics notes MOEs and indicators identical with other LOEs (covered in a previous section of the text).

geting that goes awry or causes excess civilian casualties and property destruction may not have this effect.[21]

Indicators for reductions in population expressions of support for the enemy include ambient data in the form of traditional or social media celebrations of enemy defeat or the destruction of enemy equipment. If the resources are available, polling data (especially if collected over time) can provide indicators of whether population support for the enemy is on the decline. Semistructured qualitative interviews or focus groups with members of the population can reveal similar patterns and also provide an opportunity for local nationals to express any link between precision targeting and their waning (or waxing) support for the enemy.

Reduced Materiel and Other Support to the Enemy from Population

The sense of SOF and partner-force capabilities gained from precision strikes will also, ideally, reduce the willingness of the population to join the enemy in its fight or to provide the enemy safe haven or information or materiel support of any kind—both to avoid investing in a losing battle and to avoid consequences from SOF and its partner forces. As with the previous MOE, precision strikes that go awry may, of course, not have this intended effect.

Indicators for reductions in recruitment, materiel, and other support can be found in intelligence reporting if assets are appropriately placed to monitor the enemy. Additionally, SITREPs from tactical units may note reduced population collusion with the enemy as experienced by SOF (or partner forces, if they produce SITREPs) during raids and routine patrols.

Other Possible MOEs

We did not include loss of enemy territory as an MOE for precision targeting. While the enemy may be temporarily displaced through preci-

---

[21] See Luke N. Condra, Joseph H. Felter, Radha K. Iyengar, and Jacob N. Shapiro, "The Effect of Civilian Casualties in Afghanistan and Iraq," working paper, Cambridge, Mass.: National Bureau of Economic Research, 2010, for a discussion of how civilian casualties may be linked with short-run increases in insurgent violence.

sion targeting, partner-force operations or other activities must fill this vacuum for this displacement to last.

Influence via MISO

MISO achieve influence in a variety of ways. Efforts to influence target audiences may be pursued by messaging on common media and communication platforms—ranging from the more traditional leaflets, loudspeakers, and radio or television stations to the internet through social media and other means. These efforts aim to "convey selected information and indicators to foreign audiences to influence their emotions, motives, objective reasoning, and ultimately the behavior of foreign governments, organizations, groups, and individuals."[22] Influencing emotions, motives, or reasoning are desired objectives in themselves but may also be seen as paths to achieving the ultimate objective of influencing behaviors.

PSYOP units are trained to evaluate their efforts as part of the doctrinal seven-step MISO process (planning, target audience analysis, series development, product development and design, approval, product distribution and dissemination, and evaluation). However, in practice, deployed PSYOP units may not be sufficiently staffed or have sufficient time to produce these evaluations. Nonetheless, their training familiarizes them with the development of impact and assessment criteria to determine whether they are meeting their objectives and to identify exogenous factors or "spontaneous events."[23] To produce a more manageable assessment process that is tied into the overall plan assessment, this method suggests identifying the minimum sufficient number of MOEs.

Influence via MISO has two primary objectives: (1) to reduce population support for the enemy and (2) to increase population sup-

---

[22] JP 3-13.2, 2011.

[23] JP 3-13.2, 2011. The most recent public Army doctrine is FM 3-53, 2013.

port for partners or partner forces.[24] Unlike the precision targeting LOE, in this LOE, MISO will highlight battlefield successes and also the malign and unethical activities of the enemy to decrease population support for and collusion with the enemy. As with the overlap of MOEs between partner-force and precision targeting effects, it is important during the assessment process to differentiate the *source* of these effects to the extent possible, even if the effects themselves are shared.

MOEs for This Objective

Table 3.3 lists the MOEs, which are discussed in the following subsections.

Reduced Population Expressions of Enemy Support

As previously stated, MISO are activities are designed primarily to induce changes in behavior.[25] However, MISO also aim to influence emotions, motives, and cognitive reasoning because these all play significant roles in behavioral change. Therefore, the assessment process for the influence via MISO LOE gauges changes in expressions of feeling, motive, or thought, as well as changes in behavior.

Indicators for reductions in population expressions of support for the enemy include ambient data in the form of traditional or social media celebrations of enemy defeat or the destruction of enemy equipment. If the resources are available, polling data (especially if collected over time) can provide indicators of whether population support for the enemy is on the decline. Semistructured qualitative interviews or focus groups with members of the population can reveal similar patterns and also provide the opportunity for local nationals to express any link

---

[24] As explained further in worked assessment examples, *support* includes behaviors that are supportive of partners and their objectives and/or detract from support of enemy forces and and their objectives. See Christopher Paul, Colin P. Clarke, and Beth Grill, *Victory Has a Thousand Fathers: Sources of Success in Counterinsurgency*, Santa Monica, Calif.: RAND Corporation, MG-964-OSD, 2010, for a discussion of MISO's role in strategic communication in COIN, which they find to be a frequent factor in COIN success.

[25] JP 3-13.2, 2011, pp. I-2, 3. The most recent public Army doctrine is FM 3-53, 2013.

Table 3.3
Measures of Effectiveness for Influence via Military Information Support Operations

Objective	MOE	Indicators: Operational	Indicators: Ambient	Indicators: Assessment
1. Reduce population support for the enemy	*Reduced population expressions of enemy support*		***Social and traditional media:*** *Celebrations of enemy defeat and destruction*	***Polling:*** *Endorsement of negative statements about enemy* ***Interviews:*** *Antienemy themes*
	Reduced materiel and other (e.g., intelligence, safe harbor, recruits) support to enemy from population	***Intelligence:*** *Enemy reports of reduction in recruitment, material, and other support from population* ***SITREPs:*** *Observations of less population collusion with enemy, reporting on enemy, desertions*		
2. Increase population support for partners	Increased population expressions of partner-force support		**Social and traditional media:** Positive images and text reports about partner-force operations	**Polling:** Endorsement of positive statements about partner forces **Interviews:** Pro–partner force themes
	Increased materiel and other (e.g., intelligence, safe harbor, recruits) support to partner forces from population	**Mission Tracker:** Partner force recruitment **SITREPs:** Reports of population cooperation and collaboration		

NOTE: Text in italics notes MOEs and indicators identical with other LOEs (covered in a previous section of the text).

between precision targeting and their waning (or waxing) support for the enemy.

MISO play a critical role for Objective 2 of this LOE (increase population support for partners) because newly created SOF partner forces may and require some "marketing" to encourage recruitment, acceptance, and ideally also outright support.[26]

Increased Population Expressions of Partner-Force Support

Support for partner forces is, of course, linked to the operational effectiveness and professionalism of partner forces themselves and to enemy losses due to both partner-force operations and precision targeting (see previous sections on these LOEs). Information operations will ideally provide both a trigger and a boost to positive population perceptions, whether MISO are conducted via leaflets, social media, or other channels.

As with indicators for reduction in enemy support, ambient data in the form of traditional and social media may provide indicators in the form of positive images and text endorsements of partner-force operations or recruitment events. If resources area available for polling or interviews with local nationals, these can also be used to gauge sentiment regarding partner forces. Qualitative interviews might also reveal evidence of a link between MISO and increased positive sentiment, via specific mentions of MISO content or themes.[27]

Increased Materiel and Other Support to Partner Forces from Population

Information operations can highlight and augment the operational success and "good deeds" of partner forces and can emphasize themes that resonate with the local population, such as patriotism or protect-

---

[26] See Ralph O. Baker, "The Decisive Weapon: A Brigade Combat Team Commander's Perspective on Information Operations," *Military Review*, May–June 2006, pp. 13–32, for a tactical-level account of the importance of MISO in Operation Iraqi Freedom. In particular, p. 20 includes a sample list of MOEs one unit used to assess MISO impact on both expressions of support and direct support in the form of intelligence (tips).

[27] See pp. 298–301 in Paul, Yeats, et al., 2015, for examples of how polling and surveys have been combined with qualitative data collection in past military assessments of MISO impact.

ing local values.[28] Ideally, this content will encourage active support for partner forces, including voluntary recruitment in some cases and provision of information (via tip line reports or through other means), safe harbor, or other valuable resources in other cases.

Indicators for this MOE include increases in actual recruitment numbers and in desertion rates, which will be contained in mission tracker data from tactical units involved in developing the partner force. SITREPs from tactical units (or from the partner forces themselves) may also include observations of either increased passive acceptance or outright support and cooperation with partner forces on the part of local nationals.

Other Possible MOEs

We did not include increased population support for SOF or other U.S. or coalition forces in the list of MOEs for MISO effects. In most cases, SOF will be working by, with, and through local partner forces, and the primary goal of MISO will be to bolster population approval of these forces (with U.S. and coalition forces more of a "hidden" entity). In operational environments in which positive perception of U.S. and coalition forces is an explicit goal, indicators similar to those used to gauge support for partner forces (as described earlier) can be used.

Influence via Civil Affairs Operations

The joint definition of *CAO* is

> [a]ctions planned, executed, and assessed by civil affairs forces that enhance awareness of and manage the interaction with the civil component of the operational environment; identify and mitigate underlying causes of instability within civil society; or

---

[28] See USASOC, 2017a, p. 11, for a vignette of MISO used to assist with countering the Lord's Resistance Army. Also see Paruchabutr et al., 2014, pp. IX-1–IX-4 for case study examples from Oman and the Philippines. See Paruchabutr et al., 2014, pp. VIII-5 and C-2–C-5 for a description of cultural context in SOF operational design and detailed elements of cultural factors.

> involve the application of functional specialty skills normally the responsibility of civil government.[29]

Civil affairs personnel conduct military engagement, humanitarian and civic assistance, and nation assistance to influence host-nation and foreign nation populations. Further, "CA forces assess impacts of the population and culture on military operations; assess impact of military operations on the population and culture; and facilitate interorganizational coordination."[30] SOF employs CAO in specific ways, to support core SOF missions, such as counterterrorism.[31] ARSOF CAO fill a unique role by helping stand up governance that is friendly to U.S. goals while degrading the governance activities of enemies.[32] Given this specific SOF focus, the core objectives of SOF CAO are to (1) to build effective local governance and (2) to degrade malign governance.

MOEs for This LOE

Table 3.4 lists the MOEs for this LOE.

Increased Population Expressions of Local Government Support

As SOF CA works to stand up local governance, increase its effectiveness, and establish or improve local services through the Commander's Emergency Response Program (CERP) and similar mechanisms, the population is expected to exhibit increased support for local governance and the services it provides.[33]

---

[29] JP 3-57, *Civil-Military Operations*, Washington, D.C.: Joint Staff, September 11, 2013, p. GL-6.

[30] See JP 3-57, 2013, p. xii.

[31] Linda Robinson, *The Future of US Special Operations Forces*, Washington, D.C.: Council on Foreign Relations, 2013, p. 31.

[32] Slider, 2017. Two other core capabilities include human terrain mapping and conduct of mission command. CA's governance and counter-governance functions are the key activities for operational assessment.

[33] For an extensive discussion of CERP and its economic and other impact, see Daniel Egel, Charles P. Ries, Ben Connable, Todd C. Helmus, Eric Robinson, Isaac Baruffi, Melissa A. Bradley, Kurt Card, Kathleen Loa, Sean Mann, Fernando Sedano, Stephan B. Seabrook, and Robert Stewart, *Investing in the Fight: Assessing the Use of the Commander's Emergency Response Program in Afghanistan*, Santa Monica, Calif.: RAND Corporation, RR-1508-OSD, 2016.

Table 3.4
Measures of Effectiveness for Influence via Civil Affairs Operations

Objective	MOE	Indicators		
		Operational	Ambient	Assessment
Build effective local governance	Increased population expressions of local government support		**Social and traditional media:** Positive reports or posts about local government and government services	**Polling:** Endorsement of positive statements about local government and services **Interviews:** Progovernment themes
	Increased participation in local government	**SITREPs:** Reports of engagement in local elections, attendance at government centers, and participation in civic events		
	Increased economic activity	**SITREPs:** Participation in CERP and related programs. Reports of increased market activity, uptick in construction and agriculture	**Satellite:** Increased market activity, agricultural production, electrical usage	
Degrade enemy governance	Reduced population expressions of malign governance support		**Social and traditional media:** Negative reports or posts concerning malign governance actions	**Polling:** Endorsement of negative statements about malign governance **Interviews:** Antienemy governance themes
	Decreased participation and cooperation with malign governance	**Intelligence:** Enemy reports of decreased population cooperation **SITREPs:** Observations of less population cooperation with enemy governance		

In areas with functioning traditional and social media channels, positive reports regarding local governance and services can be indicated by reports and posts. Meanwhile, polling and interviews with local nationals (if resources and security conditions permit) can provide more-systematic and deeper insights into population satisfaction with local government and services.

Increased Participation in Local Government

In some operational environments, SOF CA help stand up local governing institutions, including holding elections and setting up physical locations or events for civic participation. A logical marker of the success of these activities is the increased participation of the local population.

Indicators of increased participation are most likely to come from operational data streams. SITREPs reporting from SOF personnel who were present at governance events can help indicate level of participation in civic events and population traffic through physical locations attached to local governance.

Increased Economic Activity

SOF CA often assist with bolstering local economic paths (e.g., coordinating security for markets or agriculture) and also sponsor new development activities, such as business start-ups through CERP or similar funds. CA ties these efforts to local governance, so participation in local economic revitalization and (over the long term) increased economic activity is a logical output of CA success in this arena.

Indicators of increased economic activity can come from operational and ambient data streams. SITREPs should include reports of participation in CERP activities and observations about changes in market, agricultural, construction, or other economic activities in the area of operations. Over the long term, increases in economic activity can show up in ambient data streams; for example, satellite data can provide evidence of increased agricultural activity, the spread of electrical usage, and population migration.[34]

---

[34] For a rigorous quantitative assessment of CERP projects and their effects on these ambient indicators in Afghanistan, see Egel et al., 2016, pp. 163–176.

Reduced Population Expressions of Malign Governance Support

As SOF CA (in collaboration with partner forces) works to stand up effective local governance, it is expected that this will supplant the power vacuum filled by malign governance entities. As a result, population support for malign governance is expected to decrease.

In areas with functioning traditional and social media channels, negative posts about the undesired activities of enemy governance (taxes, forced occupation of local housing and other structures, etc.) may appear in news reports and social media posts. If security conditions and resources allow, polling and interviews with local nationals (if conducted over time) can reveal downward trends in expressions of support for enemy governance. The results of these approaches should be interpreted cautiously, however, because locals may not wish to openly express disapproval for an enemy that they fear might one day return to the area.

Decreased Participation and Cooperation with Malign Governance

Increasingly negative population sentiment toward enemy governance is also expected to affect population behavior. Specifically, the local population will comply less with demands from malign governance, such as taxes, forced occupation of residences and other structures, or participation in malign governance events designed to increase buy-in and control over the population.

Indicators for cooperation with enemy governance will come from operational data streams in the form of intelligence reporting and SITREPs. Specifically, if intelligence assets are sufficient to collect data on enemy communications, these assets will pick up reports of reduced population compliance. Similarly, SITREPs from tactical units will note observations of less population collusion with malign or shadow governance elements if tactical units are sufficiently embedded with the population and if the change is big enough to be noticed during routine patrols or other intersections with the population.

Other Possible MOEs

We did not include long-term economic stability or the establishment of a sustainable democracy as MOEs for the CAO LOE. The goal of this SOF assessment methodology is to capture and assess the effects of SOF contributions to a wider governance mission. In some cases, the governance mission is largely handled by SOF, but that is rare.

CHAPTER FOUR

Seven-Step Assessment Process

In this chapter, we propose a seven-step process for SOF operational-level assessment.[1] The intent is provide clear guidance to assessment teams on how they should organize and analyze data and communicate assessment results, which underlie any assessment framework.[2] As the goal is to develop a unified step-by-step process for developing and implementing these assessments, our approach combines elements from the six steps recommended in joint doctrine for "developing the assessment plan" and the five overall steps recommended for the execution of operation assessments.[3] The assessment approach developed and presented here is consistent with current joint doctrine; however,

---

1 Some proposed assessment processes are hierarchical, in that they are designed to consolidate the assessment efforts of subordinate headquarters (see Connable, 2012, Chapter Ten). This proposed approach assumes, given the limited headquarters capability of special operations tactical-level headquarters for assessment, that all assessment efforts of the tactical-level headquarters will be consolidated into the operational-level headquarters. If a hierarchical process is required, an approach akin to that in Connable, 2012, could be used to modify the assessment approach described here.

2 See JDN 1-15, 2015, pp. vii–viii.

3 The six recommended steps for developing the assessment plan are (1) "Gather Tools and Assessment Data"; (2) "Understand Current and Desired Conditions"; (3) "Develop Assessment Measures and Indicators"; (4) "Develop the Collection Plan"; (5) "Assign Responsibilities for Conducting Analysis and Generating Recommendations"; and (6) "Identify Feedback Mechanisms" (JDN 1-15, 2015, pp. ix–x). The five recommended steps for an operational assessment are (1) "Identify Information and Intelligence Requirements"; (2) "Develop/Modify the Assessment Plan"; (3) "Collect Information and Intelligence"; (4) "Conduct Event Based and/or Periodic Assessment"; and (5) "Provide Feedback and Recommendations" (JDN 1-15, 2015, pp. viii–ix).

we provide more-specific guidance and additional good practices for achieving rigorous results. We have also reordered doctrinal steps in some cases for methodological reasons. For example, our proposed step-by-step process also explicitly defines the development of appropriate analytical techniques for SOF assessment and provides specific guidance for informing commander decisionmaking.[4]

This report may inform further development of joint doctrine. In addition, the data collection and analytical approach developed here may inform the assessment processes of higher headquarters. At a minimum, the improved processes recommended for SOF data collection and indicator developments will facilitate provision of inputs for the higher headquarters' assessment process.

The seven-step process we propose for operational-level SOF assessments is summarized in Figure 4.1.[5] The first two steps—"determine objectives" and "identify activities"—align with the framework in Chapter Two. The following two steps—"define MOEs" and "indicators and data"—align with Chapter Three. Steps 5 and 6 describe the analysis of these data, first for each LOE and then overall, and Step 7 is a review of the assessment with the commander.

This seven-step process entails activities that should be conducted both before deployment and during operations themselves, given the importance of nesting the assessment process in both the development and execution of the operational-level plan.[6] In the seven following sections—which detail the specific activities and decisions required for each step—we therefore also highlight what needs to happen during predeployment preparation versus during deployment. We also briefly detail the challenges that an assessment team is likely to face during

[4] The development of analytical techniques is currently nested within Step 3 ("Develop Assessment Measures and Indicators") of the assessment planning and is then delegated to an assessment cell. However, our experience is that this frequently leads to the employment of ad-hoc analytical techniques because the specifics of how data will be analyzed are not explicitly developed as the data requirements are identified.

[5] We describe the alignment of these steps with existing doctrine in the corresponding sections.

[6] As an example, the very first sentence of JDN 1-15, 2015, p. i, states that "operation assessment is initiated during joint planning and executed throughout operations."

Figure 4.1
Seven Steps of Special Operations Forces Operational-Level Assessment

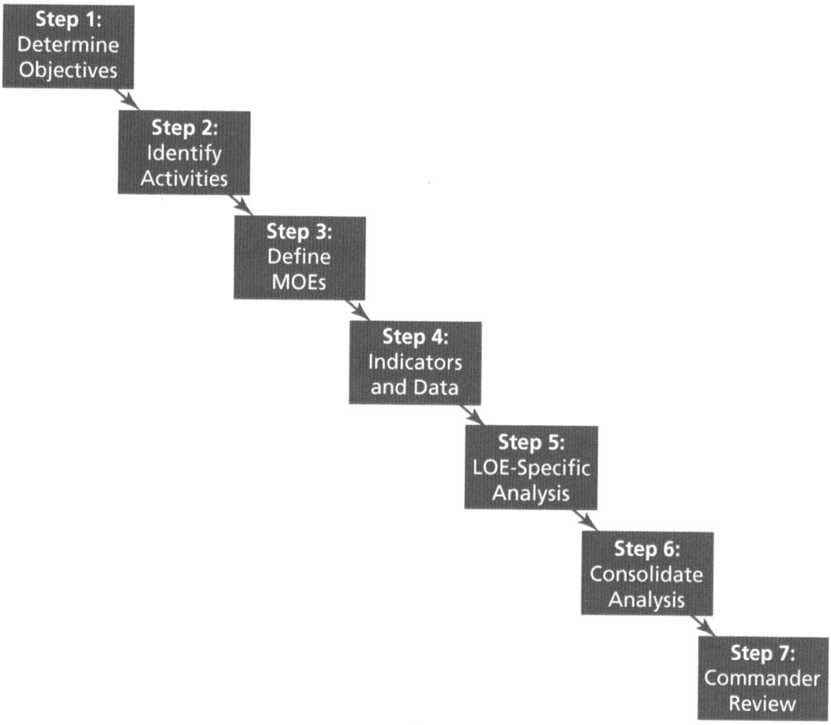

each step, and approaches for addressing these challenges. The final section provides a general implementation framework, including the timeline and frequency for assessment.

Step 1. Determine Objectives

The first step of the assessment process is to identify the key LOEs and determine the objectives of the campaign.[7] This must include a review of the commander's CONOP with a focus on the logical links

---

[7] This step is comparable to the "Identify Information and Intelligence Requirements" of the overall operation assessment and "Gather Tools and Assessment Data" of the assessment plan in JDN 1-15, 2015, pp. vii–ix.

between planned activities and the intended effects and objectives for each LOE. As part of this review, the assessment team must identify *thresholds*—lengths of time, numbers of operations, or another metric—by which objectives, interim objectives, or specific effects are expected to be seen during operations. The primary data source for this step is available documentation (e.g., plans, orders)—both from the operational-level headquarters being assessed and from higher headquarters, if applicable. It is critical that this document review be supplemented by conversations with both planners and the commander to ensure that objectives are described in discrete, measurable ways and that each objective is associated with a clear logical link between activities and effects and with a threshold by which effects are expected to be seen.

While they are identifying objectives, the assessment team must ensure that objectives are specific, measurable, achievable, relevant, and time bound (SMART).[8] The team must work to set thresholds of effects at specific time intervals that the commander believes are achievable and must ensure that there is a way to measure these effects (see Steps 3 and 4). This often will require some discussion with the command because objectives in campaign plans or other documentation may not satisfy these criteria in their original form.[9]

Predeployment: Identify Planned Campaign Lines of Effort, Objectives, and Thresholds

The assessment team delineates the specific LOEs and the objectives for them described in existing documentation. These LOEs and objectives are then reviewed with the planners and the commander for accuracy and comprehensiveness. Any gaps between the guidance of the

---

[8] See Paul, Yeats, et al., 2015, pp. 73–74.

[9] Note that the objectives in Chapter Two do not yet meet SMART criteria because generic objectives for SOF LOEs are designed to allow assessment teams to adapt them to any theater or set of SOF activities. The worked assessment example in "Atropia" in Chapter Five illustrates the process of developing SMART objectives. For another published worked example that focuses on SMART objectives, see Christopher Paul, *Assessing and Evaluating Department of Defense Efforts to Inform, Influence, and Persuade: Worked Example*, Santa Monica, Calif.: RAND Corporation, RR-809/4-OSD, 2017.

commander and the plans should be rectified by updating the relevant strategic documentation. This process may result in revised LOEs and objectives.

Two standard methods that special operations elements use can be particularly useful. First, CA units may prepare area assessments that will generate vital data and baseline understanding of the environment, key individuals, population groups, and government. Second, PSYOP units often prepare target audience analyses for key influence targets. These and other products may be used to refine LOEs, objectives, and thresholds and to derive campaign assessment MOEs, baselines from which assessments will depart, and create mission trackers (see "Step 2. Identify Activities").

Objectives should be SMART, including specific thresholds and quantifiable, measurable goals;[10] for example, "liberate at least 75 percent of villages in the south from insurgent control," or "ensure civilian freedom of movement on all major highways in the east." The combined results of achieving operational objectives should constitute the commander's desired end state.[11] Additionally, objectives must be paired with the specific activities that are expected to achieve the objectives and an expected threshold for achievement of effects; for example, "host-nation commandos will conduct clearance operations two to three times per week, liberating 10 percent of villages currently under insurgent control every month." Once objectives are paired with specific activities, the assessment team must also articulate a theory of change linking the activities with expected effects.[12] Ensuring this alignment of clear, measurable objectives with the desired end state will allow the assessment team to help brief the commander when sufficient progress has been made for assets to be deployed elsewhere and/or (later in operations) when the end state has been sufficiently achieved for

---

[10] See the discussion of "Objectives and Decision Points" in ADRP 5-0, p. 2-20. Also see JDN 1-15, 2015, p. III-6.

[11] See ADRP 5-0, p. 1-4.

[12] Assessment is an iterative process. In each assessment cycle, the team must revisit theories of change in light of new data and battlefield experience and revise these theories as needed. See Paul, 2017, pp. x, 12, 42, and 58.

operations to be scaled down in service of an exit plan. In turn, assigning thresholds to each LOE will allow the assessment team to brief the commander when expected links between operations and effects are not holding—thereby providing potential decision points for the adjustment of operations.

Deployment: Validate LOEs, Objectives, and Thresholds

As described in Chapter One, SOF operations often involve activities in remote and/or denied areas with little advance knowledge of local conditions. As a result, LOEs and objectives identified during the planning process can shift as operational experience reveals conditions that challenge assumptions about the best ways to achieve objectives or sometimes even the feasibility of objectives themselves.[13] The assessment team should revisit LOEs and objectives as new events and experiences during operations challenge: (1) the way LOEs and associated activities are expected to achieve objectives (i.e., the theory of change) or (2) the feasibility of operational objectives themselves, as well as any substantive changes to objectives or associated thresholds (i.e., timing or level of effects expected) resulting from either (1) or (2).

Challenges and Mitigation

Defining objectives that are measurable and sufficiently specific for judging success, particularly given the complex problem sets that SOF is typically deployed against, will be an ongoing challenge. Although providing a number against which to judge success will be difficult for many of these objectives, doing so is necessary and will help the command clearly understand, communicate, and assess its goals. The end state associated with objective should be reviewed with the commander and staff as part of the assessment battle rhythm, although the assessment team should track how the defined end state for each objective evolves over time. In addition, thresholds may shift as operational realities are revealed, so the assessment team should be open to modifying thresholds as new data become available.

---

[13] Paruchabutr et al., 2014, pp. I-2–I-3.

Step 2. Identify Activities

The focus of this step is on identifying and measuring the assessable activities and the ways in which they are expected to achieve objectives associated with the LOEs described in Step 1.[14] As outlined later, in "Step 5. Conduct LOE-Specific Analysis," a detailed record of SOF's activities is essential for producing statistically relevant, defensible results. Because operational-level assessments are focused on determining whether SOF is doing the right things,[15] tracking specific SOF activities is essential for providing evidence of whether these activities are helping to achieve the desired effects. We call the tool for doing this a *mission tracker*.

Collecting sufficient detail on these activities, without overburdening the tactical-level elements conducting the activities, is an essential component step. Fortunately, the requisite types of information about these activities align with the "five Ws"—who, what, where, when, and why—that are typically required of tactical-level mission planning,[16] so that tactical-level elements are likely already collecting most, if not all, of this data.

After completing an activity, tactical units should provide their perceptions of its perceived effects. This sixth kind of information is analogous to what is typically described as MOPs, although, in this case, the goal will be to capture the tactical-level element involved's self-reported performance during the activity (estimated number of enemy killed in action, independence of the local partner during operations, etc.).

Table 4.1 describes the six types of information required about an activity, and Box 4.1 provides a specific example of how these requirements would be implemented.

---

[14] This step is typically not deliberately specified in discussions of development of assessment plans but is a needed extension of Step 1.

[15] Deployable Training Division, 2013, p. 1.

[16] For example ATP 3-55.4, *Techniques for Information Collection During Operations Among Populations*, Washington, D.C.: Headquarters, Department of the Army, April 2016.

Table 4.1
Mission Tracker Requirements

Type of Information	Key Question
Who	What are the population, enemy, or friendly entities that are the "target" of the activity?
What	In what way are these entities expected to change as a result of operations?
Where	Where will this activity occur?
When	When will this activity occur?
Why	How are these activities expected to influence the target entity?
MOP	What was the perceived reach and immediate effect of the activity?

Box 4.1
Example of Activity-Specific Information

MISO leaflet drop to assist with partner operations to take back Afghan village X from insurgents in summer 2015. The leaflets contain details about insurgent atrocities or hypocrisy to help turn villagers against the insurgent force and contain additional messaging designed to encouraging desertions or weakening the will of insurgent elements to fight. The mission tracker would record the following information about this activity:

Who: Both insurgent forces and villages.

What: Decreased support for insurgents.

Where: Afghan village X (plus any geographic deviation from the planned dispersal pattern).

When: Summer 2015.

Why: Villagers' moral indignation against insurgents will be aroused by calling attention to insurgent hypocrisy and atrocities; enemy confusion and fear will be increased through warnings of their impending death.

MOP: 5,000 leaflets were dropped in a 5-km perimeter around the target village and were read by an estimated 50 villagers, based on reports from local observers.

The step-by-step process outlined in this chapter describes the important role of MOPs in a SOF operational-level assessment. MOPs provide an important intermediary in the assessment process by tracking whether the tactical elements are performing effectively. MOPs thus allow an assessment of whether the subordinate forces are doing things right, while MOEs assess whether the operational-level headquarters is doing the right things, which is the goal of an operational-level assessment.[17] For example, in a leaflet drop, MOPs would include the number of leaflets released, the approximate area in which they landed, and any immediate evidence that the population had read the leaflets.

A common approach for systematically collecting these data is a *mission tracker*, a tool frequently used by operational-level headquarters to provide situational awareness to the command. As an example, the SOJTF-Afghanistan Commander's Action Group used detailed historical data available in SOJTF-Afghanistan J3's mission tracker—which included the type, location, and time of operations SOF or its partners conducted—to conduct focused assessments of both the develop, enable, and employ partner force and precision targeting LOEs.[18] Similarly, detailed data on CERP activities, documented in the centralized Combined Information Data Network Exchange database, have been essential to assessments of this program.[19] Mission tracker data could be collected from tactical units via a standardized SITREP and then aggregated by the operational-level headquarters (see Chapter Five for more detail).

A critical component of the mission tracker is identifying a plausible relationship between activities and effects; that is, a theory of change (the "why" element in Table 4.1 and Box 4.1). This theory of change may indeed change as operations reveal unanticipated patterns or "spoilers" in the battlefield.[20] It is critical that the assessment team articulate a plausible theory of change and keep this field of the mission tracker updated as battlefield experiences challenge and refine the initial theory of change.

---

[17] Deployable Training Division, 2013, p. 1.

[18] Researchers' field experience in support of SOJTF-Afghanistan.

[19] For a detailed discussion, see Egel et al., 2016.

[20] See Osburg et al., 2014, pp. 59–60.

Predeployment: Develop Mission Tracker

Before the mission begins, standardized, parsimonious criteria for MOPs that are appropriate for the specific types of activities should be developed. A process should be in place to standardize and record incoming data from tactical-level SITREPs (see further discussion in Chapter Five). The mission tracker should also include a logical justification for how activities will achieve objectives and can provide the necessary data to track thresholds identified in Step 1.

Deployment: Validate Mission Tracker

While the mission is under way, the available mission tracker data should be reviewed, based on findings during Step 5 (analysis) and Step 6 (consolidate analysis), to validate that the criteria used for MOPs are necessary and sufficient to assess tactical performance and that the mission tracker data requirements do not place an undue burden on tactical units. The "why" of the logical connection between activities and expected effects should also be revisited. The mission tracker data should allow the assessment team to track thresholds derived from Step 1.

Challenges and Mitigation

Collecting sufficient data on relevant activities without overburdening subordinate elements and staff will require an ongoing review of these data and how they are used. While the standardized SITREP proposed in Chapter Six can streamline this process, the specific requirements of the mission tracker will need to be scaled and modified for the specific mission. Additionally, certain operational environments will make it difficult to assess the logical link between activities and effects (the "why" or theory of change field for the mission tracker). In these cases, the assessment team should brainstorm creative indicators that may provide evidence that substantiates the assumed causal path; for example, even an anecdotal account of how seeing more-effective policing convinced a resident to submit an anonymous tip can be helpful in substantiating the assumed theory of change. Assessment teams should be in frequent contact with planners and tactical units to ensure that causal assumptions between activities and effects accord with on-the-ground reality in the operational environment.

Step 3. Define MOEs

Selecting the appropriate MOEs is the focus of Step 3.[21] Determining LOEs should begin with the material from Chapter Three, which provides a template for required MOEs, by SOF LOE. Note that these LOEs, objectives, and MOEs are generic by design and are intended to be only a starting point. Campaign plans, commander's critical information requirements, and other documents may also provide specific MOEs. The assessment team must incorporate material from plans and other official documents into the LOE template provided in Chapter Three, as well as the detailed information on LOEs, objectives, and activities from Steps 1 and 2 of the assessment process. The list of assessment LOEs should also pass command review to ensure that it accords with the commander's CONOP. As part of ensuring that the assessment process meets SMART criteria, Steps 3 and 4 of the assessment process will indicate whether objectives are indeed measurable. Appendix B also describes the core criteria for MOEs: relevance, measurability, malleability, and distinctness.[22] See Chapter Five for an example of how specific operationally relevant MOEs can be derived from the generic MOEs in Chapter Two.

Predeployment: Develop MOEs

MOEs should be developed that align with Chapter Three, official documentation, and command guidance. At this phase, it is critical to ensure that MOEs line up with the measurable, quantifiable components of objectives so that the assessment team can gauge when opera-

---

[21] This step is comparable to the "Development Assessment Measures and Indicators" of the overall operation assessment, although we divide out the indicators because the types of indicators are conditional on the availability of data.

[22] Appendix B is in the companion volume: Robinson, Egel, and Brown, 2019.

tional objectives have been met. It is also critical that MOEs are constructed in such a way that the operational thresholds can be tracked.

Deployment: Review and Revalidate MOEs

The MOEs will need to incorporate any information gained during operations that requires revisions to LOEs, objectives, and activities (see Steps 1 and 2). In addition, feedback from Steps 4–6 of the assessment process that necessitates revisions of MOEs due to data constraints, analytic challenges, or command critique also needs to be incorporated. As the assessment team develops knowledge about data availability and constraints while in theater, MOEs can be revised to take advantage of data availability (as long as they are still plausibly tied to measurable objectives).

Challenges and Mitigation

The central challenge in selecting MOEs is that the set be both complete (in that it encompasses all the effects SOF is trying to achieve) and parsimonious (which is necessary to provide assessment products that the commander can readily digest). Selecting MOEs may be particularly difficult in steady-state operations because of the larger geographic area (and subregional variation) they cover, their smaller and more dispersed SOF footprint, and the longer time horizons involved. Recent experiences in Afghanistan and Iraq have demonstrated that assessment teams, encouraged to be creative in the brainstorming process, often generate hundreds of different defensible and possible MOEs. Rather than encouraging assessment teams to be creative in selecting MOEs at the outset, we recommend that the assessment team employ the standardized MOEs developed by USASOC (our proposals for these are provided in Chapter Three) and then employ creative approaches for ensuring that each MOE is (1) measured and assessed using at least two different indicators, as described in Step 4, and (2) able to provide evidence of when warning thresholds have been reached or surpassed.

Step 4. Develop Indicators and Collect Data

The next step of the assessment process involves developing a set of indicators for each MOE. Indicators must, in turn, be supported by specific data streams. The assessment team should start by developing an "ideal" set of indicators for each MOE without getting distracted by data availability. The initial list of indicators should be developed in a creative brainstorming environment. This list should then be edited and revised with a set of criteria similar to the one used to select MOEs: *relevance* (i.e., directly links with the MOE), *measurability* (i.e., can be measured with available data), *malleability* (i.e., can reasonably be expected to change within the time frame of analysis), and *distinctness* (i.e., is mutually exclusive).[23]

Next, the assessment team should search for all available (or collectable) data from military and nonmilitary sources that could be used to provide evidence for each indicator. Indicators for which no available data can be found should be removed. Assessment teams should keep a record of preferred indicators for which no data can be found. If no data can be found for any of the indicators for a specific MOE, the team will need to remove or rewrite the MOE so that it is measurable. Indicators should be revisited occasionally to determine whether new data or other considerations warrant revision.

Data Gathering

There are three different types of data: operational, ambient, and assessment. This subsection discusses each of these data types, describing their strengths and limitations. It then describes a process the assessment team should employ to select data types for inclusion.

Operational Data

Military units, and other interagency elements supporting these units, collect a multitude of data as part of their operations. These data provide geographically and temporally precise information on unit activi-

---

[23] These criteria are based on JDN 1-15, 2015, pp. II-8 and A-6. Appendix A (Robinson, Egel, and Brown, 2019) offers an expanded discussion of these and additional recommendations for how these MOEs can be developed as efficiently as possible.

ties, the operational environment, and how these are evolving. Because such data are rarely designed with assessment in mind, the key challenge in using them to support assessments is appropriately structuring the data (see Chapter Five for an extended discussion).

SITREPs, produced regularly by all military elements, are an example of an operational data source that has already demonstrated to be a powerful tool for assessing SOF.[24] At a minimum, a SITREP will include information on the position of a unit, enemy and friendly actions observed during the reporting period, and both recent and planned operations.[25] Additionally, SOF SITREPs frequently integrate data from intelligence sources on the morale of partner forces or the enemy. The use of SITREPs as a data source to support assessment, particularly given their additional value in tracking activities (see Step 2), is discussed in greater detail in Chapter Five.

A variety of other operational data sources can be used to augment SITREPs. Examples include intelligence reporting (e.g., SIGINT, HUMINT),[26] Blue force trackers,[27] and activity trackers from civilian or other elements.[28] In addition, historical data from the mission tracker itself, described in Step 2, can provide data for some MOEs (number of missions conducted by partner forces, number of key leader engagements, etc.).

Ambient Data

A wide variety of data—social media, satellite imagery, news, etc.—is typically produced and collected by other entities in environments where military operations are being conducted. Ambient sig-

---

[24] As an example, we conducted a study examining corruption among the Afghan Local Police (ALP) using historical SITREP data.

[25] FM 6-99, *U.S. Army Report and Message Formats*, Washington, D.C.: Headquarters, Department of the Army, August 19, 2013.

[26] An example of the use of intelligence is in Egel et al., 2016, which used the frequency of intelligence reporting as a proxy for enemy activity.

[27] An example of the use of Blue force tracker is in Egel et al., 2016, which used these data to measure freedom of movement of friendly forces.

[28] Key leader engagement and other data collected by the U.S. embassy's Office of Security Cooperation would be an example.

nals can require more time and effort to acquire than operational or assessment-specific data but can be powerful tools for assessing the movements, actions, and attitudes of individuals and groups.[29] For example, nighttime satellite imagery can indicate the spread (or diminishment) of electrical grid coverage;[30] imagery of smoke plumes can help track the destruction of infrastructure; and satellite data can even be used to track population movements and migration.[31] Other useful data streams that government or other entities routinely collect may present potential indicators of operational success, such as market activity or traffic flows that signal economic resurgence and/or freedom of movement.

Assessment-Specific Data

There are two types of assessment-specific data, which the military has collected since at least the Vietnam War.[32] The first type, typically referred to as *polling* or *survey* data, relies on a structured data-collection instrument in which individuals select from a list of pre-

---

[29] While some text analytics are available for some platforms (e.g., Twitter, Facebook), imagery, audio, and video data require specialized algorithms to prepare for analysis. As Chapter Five discusses in more detail, these techniques have not yet been sufficiently developed for such purposes in many cases (Olga Russakovsky, Jia Deng, Hao Su, Jonathan Krause, Sanjeev Satheesh, Sean Ma, Zhiheng Huang, Andrej Karpathy, Aditya Khosla, Michael Bernstein, Alexander C. Berg, and Li Fei-Fei, "ImageNet Large Scale Visual Recognition Challenge," *International Journal of Computer Vision*, Vol. 115, No. 3, 2015).

[30] Xi Li and Deren Li, "Can Night-Time Light Images Play a Role in Evaluating the Syrian Crisis?" *International Journal of Remote Sensing*, Vol. 35, No. 18, 2014.

[31] Francesco Checchi, Barclay T. Stewart, Jennifer J. Palmer, and Chris Grundy, "Validity and Feasibility of a Satellite Imagery-Based Method for Rapid Estimation of Displaced Populations," *International Journal of Health Geographics*, Vol. 12, No. 4, January 23, 2013.

[32] A prominent—and later controversial—example of assessment-specific data from the Vietnam War was the RAND Hamlet Evaluation System, which derived scores for medical and educational services, drinking water availability, civic action, and other elements for each village and hamlet involved in Operation Sunrise to track progress and assess elements of stability operations (Anders Sweetland, *Item Analysis of the HES (Hamlet Evaluation System)*, Santa Monica, Calif.: RAND Corporation, D-17634-ARPA/AGILE, 1968). The Hamlet Evaluation System was later criticized for producing "fabricated or irrelevant data that had no real utility at the tactical, operational, or strategic levels of operation and decision-making" (Connable, 2012, p. 131).

coded responses to a series of questions. Such polling data are typically collected through in-person or telephone interviews conducted by local national personnel or, more recently, using social media or other online platforms. The second type, unstructured interviews or focus groups, can be conducted by host nationals (e.g., civilians, partner forces) or SOF personnel; analogous data can also be collected passively.[33] Such assessment-specific data have been important to previous operational-level SOF headquarters but are typically expensive to collect and analyze, particularly because they require specialized assessment capabilities to develop and execute properly and may produce unreliable results in some operational environments in which SOF operate.[34]

Selection of Data Sets

The assessment team should begin by brainstorming all available data sets, building from the exemplars described in Chapter Three, considering each of the types of data (operational, ambient, assessment) sequentially. The data should then be evaluated against the inclusion and exclusion criteria delineated in Figure 4.2. The inclusion criteria are closely related to the inclusion criteria for MOEs (described in Chapter Three and Appendix B), a consequence of the interdependency of MOEs, indicators, and the data used to assess them. Thus, data should be *relevant*, *malleable*, and amenable to *aggregation* to support the assessment process. Of the exclusion criteria, *bias* is the most problematic because biased data can create assessment results that are incorrect and consequently cause poor or inaccurate decisionmaking; the issue of bias is discussed more fully in the "Bias Considerations"

---

[33] An example of passive collection conducted in this way was the Atmospherics Program–Afghanistan (see, for example, Chris Heatherly and Elizabeth Molnar, *The Regional Command–East Regional Information Fusion Center (RIFC) in Afghanistan*, working paper, undated).

[34] Headquarters, Combined Joint Special Operations Task Force–Afghanistan, 2011; Egel et al., 2016; and Brian Petit, "The Fight for the Village: Southern Afghanistan, 2010" *Military Review*, May–June 2011. For a discussion of some of these issues in the context of Afghanistan, see James Khalil, "The Reliability of Perception Surveys in Afghanistan," University of Sussex Institute of Development Studies, HiCN Research Design Note 15, October 2012.

Figure 4.2
Inclusion and Exclusion Criteria for Assessment Data Streams

Inclusion Criteria Consider all data that meet these requirements	• **Relevance:** Directly related to expected operational effects • **Malleable:** Can plausibly be changed within the timeframe of the operations • **Aggregation:** Can be collected with sufficient temporal and geographic precision
Exclusion Criteria Eliminate all data that meet these criteria	• **Bias:** Could provide catastrophically misleading results as a result of sampling, response, or other bias • **Inconsistency:** Cannot be collected consistently over time • **Resources:** Require expansive resources (e.g., time, money) to collect or analyze

section of Appendix B.[35] Additional exclusion criteria to consider are the possibility of *inconsistency* in the systematic collection of data and the financial *resources* needed to collect, prepare, and analyze the data. Box 4.2 gives an example of the use of these criteria.

Predeployment: Develop Indicators

The assessment team should develop and revise indicators based on information gathered in Steps 1–3, all available documentation, discussions with the command, and knowledge of available data sets. Check to ensure that indicators and data streams address the operational thresholds identified in Step 1 (which should also be present in MOEs if they are properly developed).

Deployment: Validate and Revise Indicators

Once in the operational environment, the assessment team is likely to receive information that (1) challenges assumptions about data availability, including discovery of previously unknown data streams, and/or (2) challenges prior assumptions about the relevance of specific indicators to MOEs. This new information will require revisiting and revising the relevant indicators. Of course, if key elements of opera-

---

[35] Appendix B is in the companion volume: Robinson, Egel, and Brown, 2019.

Box 4.2
Example of Inclusion-Exclusion Criteria

Use of polling data to assess the efforts of SOJTF-Afghanistan in stabilizing and protecting villages via the Village Stability Operations (VSO) and ALP programs.

Inclusion Criteria

Relevant: *Are polling data relevant to the VSO/ALP operations—that is, are they directly on the assumed causal chain linking operations to effects?* They certainly seem to be, especially if they contain answers about perceived safety, approval of district leadership, and perceptions of the efficacy of ALP.

Malleable: *Are polling data sufficiently malleable—that is, can they be expected to change at the rate of operations and their effects?* Perceptions can certainly change rapidly, so the malleability criterion has been met, at least in theory.

Aggregation: *Can data be collected with the desired frequency and geographic precision?* Polling data may only be feasibly collected every quarter—due to the time required, funding available, and polling team safety concerns. SOF operations in villages (and their effects on perceptions of villagers) could change more rapidly than quarterly, so this raises one red flag. Polling responses may be obtained only at the district level, without any confidence of what villages the program was being conducted in. This raises another red flag because VSO operations were conducted at a highly local level.

Exclusion Criteria

Bias: *Do polling data show potentially fatal problems with bias?* There are some obvious sources of bias that come to mind immediately.[a] Do polling respondents trust the team administering the polls, and do they feel safe enough to provide honest answers? In areas in the midst of heavy conflict, this is doubtful. Do the questions we want to ask make sense in another language and another cultural mindset? It is possible that, particularly in war-torn areas with long histories of conflict, security means different something different from what it might mean to us? So, bias raises a red flag here as well. The risk of sample bias is greater in conflict zones and areas of low economic development.

Inconsistency: *Can data be collected systematically over time?* Respondents who do not understand the questions that are being asked might be responding fairly randomly or using different frames of reference each time they answer the question. If data might change because of this type of error, data consistency is a potential problem.

Resources: *What resources are needed?* Collecting polling data from thousands of respondents in remote, war-torn areas comes at a high price (including personal risk to the polling team). It is important to consider whether the resulting benefits for operational assessment are worth this price, especially given the multiple red flags outlined above.

Summary

If other data, more precise and easier to collect data, are not available to measure local perceptions, polling should be considered. Other data sources (e.g., SITREPs, HUMINT, SIGINT) may provide similar results without the financial costs and risk to civilian personnel.

[a] See Khalil, 2012, for an extended discussion.

tions change, such as the assumed causal connection between activities and objectives or a change in the commander's intent and objectives, MOEs and their supporting indicators and data streams will also need to be adjusted.

Challenges and Mitigation

The central tension in the development of indicators is the trade-off between quantitative and qualitative measurement approaches. In general, there is a perception that quantitative measures are preferred because they are less susceptible to subjective interpretation. However, the first cautionary note cited in the assessment appendix of joint planning doctrine states: "The presence of numbers or mathematical formulae in an assessment does not imply deterministic certainty, rigor, or quality."[36] While quantitative indicators may be helpful, caution should be exercised so not to create false certainty based on "junk arithmetic" that makes sweeping assumptions or even guesses when assigning numeric values to complex, multifaceted phenomena.[37] When possible, the assessment team should include both quantitative and qualitative indicators, *triangulating* across the "rigor" quantitative indicators offer and the more nuanced understanding qualitative measures can provide.

Step 5. Conduct LOE-Specific Analysis

Analysis of the data identified in Step 4 for each LOE involves selecting the appropriate analytic method, executing the analysis, and critiquing and reviewing the findings. A core element of assessment is identifying change over time, which requires comparison with a baseline assessment (and/or previous assessments conducted).[38] Thus, the assessment team must select analytic techniques that are able to detect change

---

[36] JP 5-0, 2017 p. VI-20.

[37] For a discussion of these risks, and how to create reliable quantitative scores for assessment purposes, see Upshur et al., 2012. See also Connable, 2012, p. 90.

[38] See JDN 1-15, 2015, p. viii, I-6, I-10, II10, and A-7. Also see Paul, Yeats, et al., 2015, pp. 33–35.

from the baseline point of measurements. In some cases, units will assess the country, regional, or local context before deployment. While this is useful for operational planning and general situational awareness, the true baseline will often be the first measurement of the environment conducted while in country or the last assessment conducted by the previous unit deployed to the area.

Analytical Techniques

There are three major analytical techniques that the assessment team can draw on to identify change from the baseline assessment and over time—qualitative, quantitative, and triangulation (also often referred to as mixed methods)—which we describe in this section.[39] Each of these methods will be appropriate in some settings—the ideal type of method is typically driven by the background of the assessment team, the type of data available, and the requirements of the audience[40]—although all methods offer statistically defensible findings,[41] as we will describe. However, whenever possible, we recommend using triangulation—i.e., employing multiple data sources and analytical approaches—whenever possible.

Qualitative

When there are relatively few data points—typically described as *small-N studies*—qualitative tools are typically the first and best option. Qualitative analysis typically involves systematic review of existing data, identifying either trends or themes. The main criticism of qualitative methods is that they do not typically employ research designs that admit causal, statistically relevant interpretations.[42] However, qualitative research methods based on ideas from statistical theory

[39] For more detail, see Appendix A in the companion volume: Robinson, Egel, and Brown, 2019.

[40] For example, John W. Creswell, *Research Design: Qualitative, Quantitative, and Mixed Methods Approaches*, Thousand Oaks, Calif.: SAGE Publications, 2013.

[41] For example, Henry E. Brady and David Collier, Rethinking Social Inquiry: Diverse Tools, Shared Standards, Lanham, Md.: Rowman & Littlefield Publishers, 2004.

[42] For example, Gary King, Robert O. Keohane, and Sidney Verba, *Designing Social Inquiry: Scientific Inference in Qualitative Research*, Princeton, N.J.: Princeton University Press, 1994.

are available; as an example, process tracing can establish potential causal mechanisms by using formal logical tests to rule out competing hypotheses and establish causal narratives.[43]

Qualitative approaches are particularly useful when there are a large number of "unknown unknowns" in the operating environment. The exploratory nature of such approaches can be used to develop better overall knowledge of the operational environment and to discover unanticipated actors and processes. For example, qualitative interviews with SOF trainers or partner forces themselves help explain why partner-force recruitment, retention, and battlefield performance are particularly high among a certain ethnicity or tribe. Similarly, the process-tracing approach is appropriate when there is little knowledge of cause and effect processes in the operating environment. This approach can be used to sort out competing causal theories about the link between SOF activities (and the activities of others) and desired effects.

Quantitative

Quantitative analysis is the most appropriate analytical technique when highly structured data with a large number of data points are available. Quantitative approaches focus on the measurement of correlations between different variables, with analysis seeking to identify potential causal mechanisms between those variables. Though ubiquitous among assessments, both military and otherwise, as a consequence of their convincing statistical results, quantitative analyses are particularly prone to analytical bias (as described in Appendix A[44]).

Quantitative analysis is most appropriate for SOF assessments when the assessment team is assured of the validity and reliability of quantitative data and have a clear idea of the relationship between SOF activities and effects. For example, a quantitative analysis of partner-

[43] For more details and a worked example, see David Collier, "Understanding Process Tracing," *Political Science & Politics*, Vol. 44, No. 4, 2011.

[44] For more detail, see Appendix A in the companion volume: Robinson, Egel, and Brown, 2019.

force operations on enemy territorial loss would be useful if reliable and valid data were available on both variables.

Mixed Methods

The most effective assessments typically incorporate a blend of tools to provide both precision and insight, although operational assessments have historically struggled to achieve the appropriate mix.[45] The best possible analytical approach, which should be employed whenever appropriate data are available, is the use of both quantitative and qualitative analytic techniques—referred to in the academic literature as *mixed methods*.[46]

Analysis is typically conducted iteratively, with the qualitative analysis generating hypotheses that are then tested using quantitative data,[47] and vice versa. Triangulation gives causally defensible results only if either the qualitative or quantitative methods themselves give such results. However, triangulation provides a means of revealing plausible relationships between activities and effects when causal analyses are not otherwise possible.[48] This approach can be particularly powerful for assessments of SOF—e.g., combining qualitative analysis of interviews, intelligence reporting, and partner-force reporting with quantitative analysis of polling data can provide a determination of whether SOF played a decisive role in stability operations within a region.

---

[45] Mushen and Schroden, 2014, p. 34.

[46] R. Burke Johnson, Anthony J Onwuegbuzie, and Lisa A Turner, "Toward a Definition of Mixed Methods Research," *Journal of Mixed Methods Research*, Vol. 1, No. 2, April 2007; Michael Quinn Patton, "Enhancing the Quality and Credibility of Qualitative Analysis," *Health Services Research*, Vol. 34, No. 5, Pt. 2, December 1999.

[47] This is the approach Egel et al., 2016, employed, using interviews with SOF operators to generate hypotheses that are then validated using available quantitative data.

[48] For a worked example of using triangulation to derive a complex causal story, see Ryan A. Brown, David P. Kennedy, Joan S. Tucker, Daniela Golinelli, and Suzanne L. Wenzel, "Monogamy on the Street: A Mixed-Methods Study of Homeless Men," *Journal of Mixed Methods Research*, Vol. 7, No. 4, October 2013.

Figure 4.3
Analytic Considerations for Assessment

Data match	• Does the analytic technique match the nature of the data? • If not, can data be restructured without too much loss of fidelity?
Analytic sensitivity	• Is the analytic technique highly sensitive to minor tweaks or manipulations by the analyst? • Does the analytic technique tend to oversuggest the relevance or importance of themes or variables?
Exploration and discovery	• Does the analytic approach allow for sufficient exploration of the data? That is, can it discover unknown unknowns? • If not, can another technique be added for this purpose?
Causal inference	• Does the approach allow ruling out alternative hypotheses or even confirmation of a working hypothesis?

Review Selected Approaches

After determining an analytical approach, four sequential steps should be used to validate the approach, as summarized in Figure 4.3.[49]

The first two of these steps focus on validating the appropriateness of the techniques employed. The first—data match—ensures that the analysis is appropriate for the data being used, including the amount of structure in the data, the quantity of data available, and the frequency of the data. The second—analytic sensitivity—examines the robustness of the analytical approach by examining how small changes in the approach (e.g., adding or subtracting variables, filtering out a small number of observations) could lead to large changes in results.[50]

---

[49] The discussion of analytical methods in Appendix A (Robinson, Egel, and Brown, 2019) provides additional details on the types of risks that can be encountered with each type of analytic method and how to overcome them.

[50] This concern is particularly problematic in quantitative analyses with relatively few observations; see, e.g., Samprit Chatterjee and Ali S. Hadi, *Sensitivity Analysis in Linear Regression*,

The third and fourth steps of the validation process focus on the completeness of the analysis—i.e., determining whether there are additional techniques that could be employed to strengthen the analysis. The exploration and discovery step focuses on whether there are sufficient data to generate new hypotheses and to identify unexpected factors that might be called "unknown and unknowns."[51] The final test is whether there are methods that can provide causal certainty—these could include process tracing, triangulation, or quasi-experimental methods, as described earlier.

Predeployment: Develop Analytical Approach

Before deploying, the assessment team should use its existing knowledge of LOEs, objectives, activities, indicators, and data streams (results of Steps 1–5 of the assessment process) to select the most appropriate analytic techniques to test the association of SOF activities with effects for each LOE. In some cases, the number of MOEs and indicators per LOE will necessitate more than one analytic method. The team should ensure that the analytic process is set up to detect when warning thresholds have been reached.

Deployment: Review Approach and Revalidate, If Necessary

As illustrated in Box 4.3, the analysis process itself can prompt the need for modifications to analytic techniques (or even entirely new techniques), and this is difficult to predict before deploying and conducting the first analyses. After the first assessment analysis and briefing with the commander, the assessment team should revise analytic

---

Hoboken, N.J.: John Wiley & Sons, 2009; Michael A. Babyak, "What You See May Not Be What You Get: A Brief, Nontechnical Introduction to Overfitting in Regression-Type Models," *Psychosomatic Medicine*, Vol. 66, No. 3, 2004.

[51] Both qualitative and quantitative methods—e.g., machine-learning, exploratory statistical analysis—can be employed for this kind of analysis; see Indranil Bose and Radha K. Mahapatra, "Business Data Mining—A Machine Learning Perspective," *Information & Management*, Vol. 39, No. 3, December 2001; Carolin Strobl, James Malley, and Gerhard Tutz, "An Introduction to Recursive Partitioning: Rationale, Application, and Characteristics of Classification and Regression Trees, Bagging, and Random Forests," *Psychological Methods*, Vol. 14, No. 4, December 2009, p. 323.

Box 4.3
Example of Review of Analytic Process

Correlation of the timing and size of partner-force operations with enemy territorial loss.

Data Match

Does the analytic technique match the nature of the data? At first glance, correlation seems to make sense. However, closer examination of data on enemy territory reveals that it is coded as shapes drawn on a map, with qualifications about how much control the enemy has in each area noted by the color of the lines for each shape. This is not immediately amenable to quantitative analysis.

If not, can data be restructured without losing too much fidelity? Yes. The assessment team developed a process of drawing geometric shapes on top of the maps roughly approximating each shape, then using geometric equations to calculate the amount of space within each shape. In addition, the team weighted the value of each shape so that (for example) a shape on top of an area noted as "70% enemy controlled" was counted as 70 percent of the territory.

Analytic Sensitivity

Is the analytic technique highly sensitive to minor tweaks or manipulations by the analyst? During data cleaning and initial analytic tests, the assessment team noticed that correlation coefficients changed drastically when including or excluding two of the largest partner operations.

Does the analytic technique tend to "oversuggest" the relevance or importance of themes or variables? In this case, the assessment team found a strong relationship between partner-force operations and enemy territorial loss but only when including the two large operations mentioned above. The team noted that its regression coefficient might be overstating the overall relationship.

Exploration and Discovery

Does the analytic approach allow sufficient exploration of the data? That is, can it discover "unknown unknowns"? As described above, the team noticed the strong effect of the two large outlier cases but was unable to determine why these operations drove so much of the effect. Members brainstormed about possible ways to get a more-nuanced understanding.

If not, can another technique be added for this purpose? The assessment team went back to the data and coded each operation for the specific partner-force unit involved and also the nature of SOF enablers for each partner-force operation. The team was able to discover a deeper pattern in the data: Two of the five partner-force units regularly received close air support (CAS) during partner operations and were able to leverage CAS for particularly effective clearing operations against the enemy. This pattern was present only for large, multiday operations, those that involved the two "top performer" partner-force units, and those that involved significant CAS.

(continued)

Box 4.3—Continued

Causal Inference

Does the approach allow the team to rule out alternative hypotheses or even confirm a working hypothesis? With the additional variables on the partner-force unit and CAS, the assessment team was able to gain a more-nuanced understanding of the possible factors driving the relationship between partner-force operations and enemy territorial loss evidenced by the initial correlation they found. However, they also noticed that the two top performing partner-force units were the only ones that received CAS during their operations in the single quarter of data on hand. Thus, it was impossible to determine whether the other partner forces might also be able to incur significant enemy territorial losses with the addition of CAS. The team resolved to mention this to the command and to revisit the analysis with additional data (ideally including more-balanced provision of CAS across partner-force units).

Summary

Correlation analysis was appropriate for this analysis, although it required some moderately labor-intensive data formatting and cleaning. The assessment team encountered some limitations with causal inference that could be addressed with more data. However, if additional data do not include a more mixed distribution of CAS across partner-force units, other analytic approaches (particularly qualitative techniques) might be required to gain additional insight.

techniques in response to (1) issues noticed during analysis and (2) the degree to which results briefed to the command were defensible and sufficient to guide further operational decisionmaking for each LOE.

Challenges and Mitigation

Assessment teams face two central, and interrelated, challenges: ensuring objectivity and finding sufficient time to conduct careful analysis. Our recommended approach for simultaneously addressing both challenges is to prespecify the analytical methods that will be used for the assessment—which is a recent good practice from the humanitarian assistance assessment community—and then update the analytical approaches only on a quarterly basis, as part of the review process. In addition to facilitating the assessment process, this standardization of assessment would allow elements based in the United States or elsewhere to support assessment of deployed headquarters.

Figure 4.4
Expanding Sphere of Influence on Jolo Island, 2006–2007

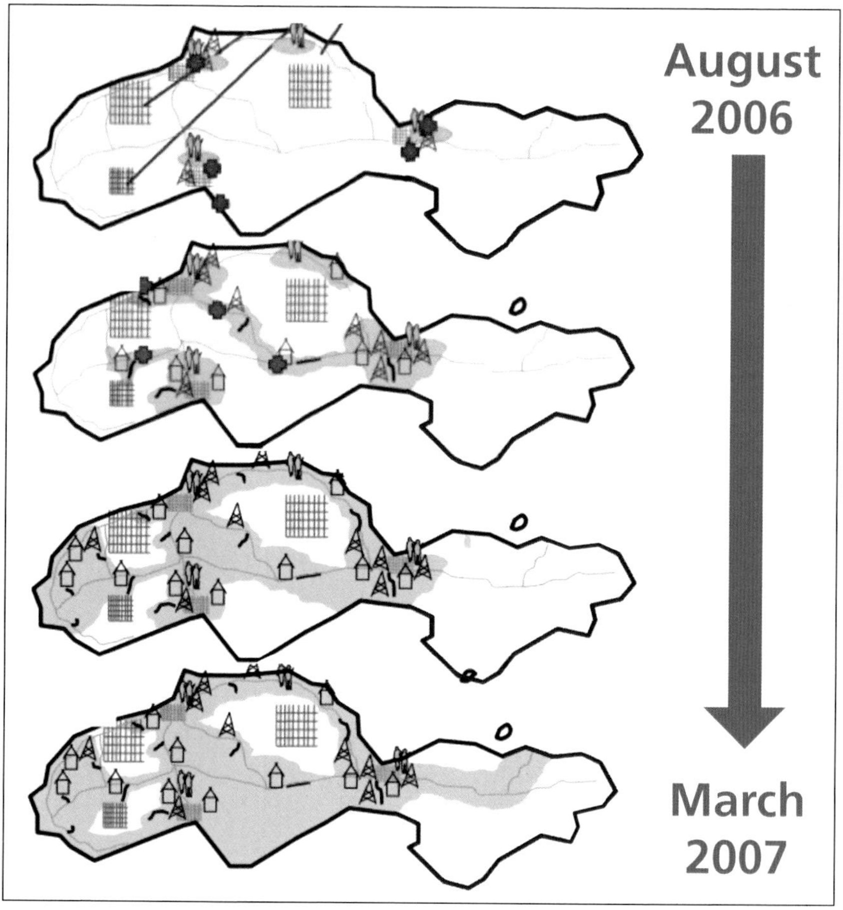

SOURCE: Composite from Joint Special Operations Task Force–Philippines, "JSOTF-P Overview," briefing slides, 2008.
NOTE: Green area indicates sphere of influence.

Step 6. Consolidate Analysis

The assessment process is detailed, complex, and labor-intensive; in many cases, weeks or even months of labor are required to produce a single report. In some cases, the team will need to summarize assessment results across a considerable period and across LOEs for an efficient briefing to the command or external audiences. These reports must, of course, be tailored to the needs and interests of each audience. For reporting to higher levels of command and audiences with oversight responsibility, preparing a concise presentation that consolidates insights across LOEs is critical for communicating the overall effectiveness of the operational-level headquarters' plan.

We recommend that this briefing product have two types of information. First, because a central goal of the assessment is to provide the data that a commander can use for optimizing the operational plan, briefing slides should provide summaries of the results obtained for each of the LOEs using the approach described in Step 5. This step also involves having the assessment team examine trends or patterns of data for each LOE and pointing out anomalies or irregularities to the commander (e.g., a top-performing unit or region is suddenly doing much worse than expected), presenting the commander with potential decision points for adjustments to operations or reallocation of assets.

Second, this briefing should include a visualization that enables the commander to see all LOE-specific results in relation to each other, to capture the overall trajectory of the campaign's multiple LOEs. A map—displaying overall changes in conditions attributable to SOF—will often be the most appropriate approach for visualizing this summary measure in most circumstances. Figure 4.4 illustrates this approach, summarizing the progress of an operational-level SOF element in the Philippines using a single summary metric—in this case, the change in self-reported sphere of influence of the U.S. SOF personnel on the ground.[52] In many operations, an analogous self-reported sphere of influence—gathered from tactical elements via standardized SITREPs (see Chapter Six)—can also be a powerful summary measure. In either case, it is important to note that additional overlays (power grid, roads, village locations, etc.) are important to qualify whether territory controlled is useful or has strategic value.

A second approach, for use when data akin to these sphere-of-influence data are not available, would be to create a composite measure

---

[52] Joint Special Operations Task Force–Philippines refers to these as *liaison coordination elements*.

that overlays all LOE-specific analyses overlaid in a geographic way.[53] Although this is technically more challenging than the approaches previously discussed, development professionals have developed off-the-shelf tools for constructing maps in similar limited-data situations.[54] This composite map could be constructed using these methods in three steps. First, the analysis described in Step 5 would be conducted for each LOE. Second, the findings for each LOE would be extrapolated across the geographic features based on observable characteristics. If desired, these LOE-specific maps could be averaged together to create a single overall measure, but efforts to create an overarching summary measure are fraught with challenges and interpretive pitfalls.[55]

As part of the consolidated analysis, the assessment team should prepare a slide for the commander describing observations or data trends that indicate LOEs are influencing each other to achieve or obstruct objectives. Some interactions among LOEs will have been anticipated during the operational and assessment planning process, while other cross-LOE influences will be detected by the assessment team while analyzing results in theater.[56] Additionally, this briefing should include at least one slide describing hidden complexity, uncertainty, and caveats to the summarized analysis to make the audience aware of hidden variations that the summary briefing has glossed over.

---

[53] The creation of similar maps is now popular in predictive policing and has been shown to be a useful tool for supporting police operations (e.g., Walter L. Perry, Brian McInnis, Carter C. Price, Susan C. Smith, and John S. Hollywood, *Predicative Policing: The Role of Crime Forecasting in Law Enforcement Operations*, Santa Monica, Calif.: RAND Corporation, RR-233-NIJ, 2013).

[54] World Bank, "Software for Poverty Mapping," August 11, 2016.

[55] There may be a temptation to try to create a model to assemble these in some optimal ways. However, joint doctrine discourages the use of weights (e.g., JDN 1-15, 2015, p. A-2), and the analytical tools for combining data and indicators for a variety of LOEs in a sophisticated way are still nascent (e.g., the difficulty of the cultural geography model described in Ben Connable, Walter L. Perry, Abby Doll, Natasha Lander, and Dan Madden, *Modeling, Simulation, and Operations Analysis in Afghanistan and Iraq: Operational Vignettes, Lessons Learned, and a Survey of Selected Efforts*, Santa Monica, Calif.: RAND Corporation, RR-382-OSD, 2014, is emblematic of these challenges).

[56] These complex interactions usually cannot be assessed systematically in a quantitative fashion but are revealed by specific incidents and anecdotes from tactical reporting.

Predeployment

Before deploying, the assessment team should draft a composite assessment briefing, including a map-based geographic component. As part of this planning process, the team should draft possible results (these can be made up without data). The team should practice displaying these results in the draft format for the commander assessment briefing. Because MOEs must be properly aligned with (measurable) objectives, this briefing should provide the commander with indications of progress made toward these operational objectives and any new cross-LOE influences detected. The assessment team should also summarize progress across operational objectives to illustrate progress toward the commander's desired end state. The team also must determine when and how it will provide information about warning thresholds that have been reached or surpassed during operations.

Deployment

During deployment, the assessment team should be attentive both to changes in the commander's intent (and associated objectives) and to new patterns in the data indicating cross-LOE effects. While some socialization of assessment results will ideally be shared in an ongoing way, the first briefing to the commander will be a learning experience for both the assessment team and the commander and his staff. The consolidated assessment results should be briefed in a "bottom line up front" format, with backup slides describing data sources, analytic processes, and more detailed results as needed. This briefing can be used to modify the assessment process and outputs (see Chapter Five).

Challenges and Mitigation

Developing appropriate summary measures for SOF efforts that are dominated by a single LOE is relatively straightforward—and can build on existing techniques described earlier—but developing a composite picture that captures the combined effects of SOF operations and the interdependencies between LOEs in multi-LOE operations is more difficult.

Emerging technologies that provide real-time visualizations of complex data now offer tools for overcoming this challenge for the first time—e.g., newly developed glyph-based techniques can provide visualizations of multivariate data with a spatial component.[57] These approaches would allow visualizations of assessment data comparable to what commanders use for viewing operational data (feeds from unmanned aerial vehicles, etc.). There is not yet a preferred approach for this, but we anticipate that these techniques will evolve rapidly in the coming years. Until a standardized approach that is applicable across all problem sets is developed, the assessment team should coordinate with the J6 to provide the commander as broad a set of visualization options as possible during predeployment so that he might select an approach that is most appropriate to the needs of the command.

Step 7. Commander Review

The ultimate authority on SOF activities and effects rests with the commander and his subordinate elements. The assessment team must work with the command, campaign planners, and other staff members to ensure that they understand the theater- and campaign-specific nuances of LOEs, operational objectives, and SOF activities and how these activities are expected to achieve their effects. Thus, the final step in the assessment process is a deliberate review of all steps of the assessment plan with the commander and staff. This will allow the team to validate the LOEs, objectives, activities, MOEs, indicators, data streams, and analytic processes planned to see whether the commander and his staff notice (1) internal inconsistencies, (2) inconsistencies with the command's CONOP, or (3) inconsistencies with constraints or conditions in theater. The review will also allow the assessment team to describe the format and types of results that its analyses will yield, which will allow the command to provide initial feedback on whether this will be useful to guide operational decisionmaking.

---

[57] Rita Borgo, Johannes Kehrer, David Chung, Eamonn Maguire, Robert S. Laramee, Helwig Hauser, Matthew Ward, and Min Chen, "Glyph-Based Visualization: Foundations, Design Guidelines, Techniques and Applications," paper presented at Eurographics 2013, Girona, Spain, May 6–10, 2013. For a worked example for Syria, see SynGlyphX, "Syria: Crisis in Context," video, 2017.

Predeployment: Develop Assessment Approach

As described earlier, after completing Steps 1–6 of the assessment process, the assessment team should brief the assessment plan to the commander and his staff. This will likely result in revisions based on feedback from the command on the internal logic, feasibility, and operational usefulness of the assessment plan. Establishing a clear analytic plan before deployment will help ensure some degree of objectivity, even if analytic processes must later be adapted to data availability or other constraints in theater.

Deployment: Review Approach and Revalidate, If Necessary

After the first major briefing to the command, the assessment team should conduct a full review of the strengths and weaknesses of all assessment components. Thus, it should review (and repeat, if needed) Steps 1–6, which will allow a review of LOEs, objectives, activities, MOEs, indicators, data streams, and analytic processes. Any changes for the next assessment period should be briefed to the command for comments and approval.

Challenges and Mitigation

Ensuring that the assessment can determine (1) when the mission is complete and (2) when operations are either unproductive or counterproductive, and operational-level changes are required, will be an ongoing challenge for the assessment team. As part of this commander review, the assessment team needs to begin by reviewing the commander's previous guidance about key decision criteria (discussed in Step 1), complemented with the use of warning thresholds throughout the assessment process, then advise the commander on whether these failure or success conditions have been satisfied. The team will need to assess the relative permanence of the results achieved and identify leading indicators of backsliding or reversal of gains. The commander can then decide how to update the operational approach or assessment criteria.

Implementation

Operational assessments are designed to be fully integrated into both operational planning and the commander's decisionmaking cycle.[58] These assessments are therefore "initiated during joint planning and executed throughout operations."[59] Accordingly, some official publications suggest that the assessment cell or assessment working group be located directly with the J3 or J5.[60] Furthermore, joint doctrine defines operational assessment as a

> continuous process to determine the overall effectiveness of employing joint force capabilities during military operations by measuring the progress toward accomplishing a task, creating a condition or effect, or achieving an objective that supports decision making to make operations more effective.[61]

Thus, the assessment process must be initiated early (predeployment), continuously active, and both integrated with and responsive to the command.

There are three broad predeployment assessment phases. The first is the formation of the assessment team, which should be done soon after the establishment of the primary command elements to ensure that the assessment process is nested with planning. The second is the development of the assessment process itself, following the seven steps outlined earlier, and repeating Steps 1–5 as needed (as described in Step 6). The final step is the socialization of the plan with the rest of the command—e.g., J2, J3, J5, and J6—to ensure that needed data collection and relevant systems are in place to support the assessment process. These steps, as well as the appropriate organizational position-

---

58 U.S. Army War College, 2016; ATP 5-0.3, 2015. For SOF-specific guidance on assessment and its relationship to operational decisionmaking, see Paruchabutr et al., 2014.

59 JDN 1-15, 2015, p. i.

60 See JDN 1-15, 2015, for a discussion of different structural locations for the assessment cell and the trade-offs associated with each. For further guidance on setting up an assessment cell, see Joint Staff, 2011, pp. IV-7–IV-8.

61 ATP 5-0.3, 2015, p. 85.

Figure 4.5
Assessment Battle Rhythm

Predeployment	1: Create assessment team 2: Develop assessment process (Steps 1–6) 3: Gain command approval and support for process
Deployment	• Weekly – Update mission tracker • Monthly – Update and code quantitative and qualitative data streams – Link MOEs to activities and conduct statistical analysis • Quarterly – Brief command on findings – Update assessment framework

ing and manning of the assessment team, can help ensure that the assessment process is integrated with operational decisionmaking, as opposed to a marginalized or peripheral activity.[62]

The appropriate frequency of assessments depends on the pace of operations and on the command's needs and the commander's rhythm of decisionmaking. While assessment briefings are often quarterly,[63] updates may be required as frequently as monthly, weekly, or even daily in some cases.[64] A small assessment team will likely be unable to produce full assessments more frequently than quarterly. Therefore, Figure 4.5 illustrates both predeployment steps and a suggested deployment battle rhythm for assessment based on a quarterly briefing cycle. When operations or the environment are changing particularly rapidly or when more-frequent updates are required for fast operational decisionmaking, a monthly or even biweekly assessment rhythm may be preferred.

---

[62] See discussions in Jonathan Schroden, "Why Operations Assessments Fail: It's Not Just the Metrics," *Naval War College Review*, Vol. 64, No. 4, Autumn 2011, and Paul, Yeats, et al., 2015, Chapter Four.

[63] For example, ATP 5-0.3, 2015 assumes a quarterly interval for operational-level assessment.

[64] See Joint Staff, 2011, p. V-3.

Assessment tasks while deployed can similarly be divided into three phases. The first, which should occur weekly, is the update of data on the types of activities being conducted (corresponding to Step 2)—verify accuracy of the mission tracker, accessing appropriate tactical-level SITREPs, etc. The second, which should occur monthly, are the update of all relevant indicator data (corresponding to Steps 3 and 4) and analysis of the data to produce intermediary assessment products (corresponding to Step 5). Finally, once per quarter, the results from the assessment process should be briefed to the command group (corresponding to Step 6), then all steps of the assessment process should be reviewed and updated, if necessary, to reflect an evolving operating environment or additional guidance from higher commands. While it is important that the SOF assessment process serve the SOF operational commander's needs, a clear and concise assessment of SOF operational effects will also make it easier for higher headquarters to judge how SOF is contributing to the larger fight.

This chapter provided the overall SOF assessment process, with specific examples in boxes. The following chapter illustrates the seven-step process with a fictitious example operational from the simulated "Atropia" environment. It thus provides a fuller illustration of how an assessment team might work through each step.

CHAPTER FIVE

Sample Assessment

This chapter describes our proposed assessment process using the well-worn fictional example of a conflict between Atropia and Ariana.[1] We situate ourselves as the assessment team recruited by the newly formed Special Operations Joint Task Force—Atropia (SOJTF-Atropia), which is preparing to deploy to Baku, Atropia.

Scenario: Atropia

Conflict between Atropia and Ariana is escalating. Atropia, a strategic ally of the United States, given its leadership role in the Western-friendly Caspian Federation, has faced rising instability in its southern territories, which are dominated by ethnic Arianas, over the past decade. This instability has been blamed on the South Atropian People's Party (SAPA), an insurgent element composed of ethnic Arianas who were trained and equipped in neighboring Ariana. SAPA has been implicated in attacks against Atropian Army (AA) units and the destruction of physical infrastructure (e.g., roads, water pipelines) across the southern territories.

Although this insurgency has been slowly growing in strength, simultaneous attacks last month on the British and Canadian embassies in Atropia's capital of Baku—committed by an unknown terrorist organization—have shocked the Atropians and the world. In the

[1] The scenario in this chapter is built around a publicly downloadable Atropia scenario (U.S. Army, "Warrior Forge 2012: The Road to War," 2012).

face of both overt saber-rattling by the Arianas, with Ariana military units violating Atropia's southern border and suspected covert action by Ariana Special Purpose Forces, the Atropians recently requested military support from the United States.

The U.S. Secretary of Defense is requesting that a Special Operations Joint Task Force—Atropia (SOJTF-Atropia) deploy to Baku, Atropia, to support the Atropian government. The SOJTF-Atropia commander has developed an operational plan with the following interrelated LOEs:

- *LOE 1: Develop, enable, and employ partner force.* SOF will support Atropia's security forces in three ways: (1) train Atropia's primary COIN force, the Atropian Special Forces (ASF); (2) provide operational advice and enablers to the ASF in support of COIN operations against SAPA;[2] and (3) conduct battalion-level training with AA units.
- *LOE 2: Precision targeting.* SOF will conduct unilateral counter-network operations to identify and neutralize terrorist threats against international targets in Baku.
- *LOE 3: Influence via MISO.* SOF will conduct unilateral and partnered MISO using pamphlets, radio, and television shows to strengthen support for the Atropia government and decrease support for factions loyal to Ariana in southern territories and along the southern border.
- *LOE 4: Influence via CAO.* SOF will conduct unilateral and partnered CAO—in coordination with the U.S. Agency for International Development (USAID) and other development agencies, if feasible—focused in the southern territories.

[2] This support is analogous to that provided by JSOTF-P (e.g., Robinson, Johnston, and Oak, 2016, p. 1).

Step 1. Determine Objectives

The assessment team received notification on December 1, 2019, that SOJTF-Atropia would deploy to Baku, Atropia, on March 1, 2020, for 18 months in support of Operation Western Peace. This gave the assessment team three months to review operational documents and determine the primary objectives for the SOJTF-Atropia LOEs. The team cross-referenced guidance on the general objectives for each LOE (see Chapter Three) with these operational documents and conversations with planners and other command staff to produce the following list of objectives by SOJTF-Atropia LOEs:

- LOE 1: Develop, enable, and employ partner force.
  - *Objective 1:* SOF builds and sustains a single company of ASF by December 1, 2020, building toward a full ASF battalion (three ASF companies) by January 1, 2022. SOF is expected to complete training of three ASF Operational Detachment Alphas (ODAs) by August 2020.
  - *Objective 2:* SOF supports ASF COIN operations in southern Atropia against SAPA to retake territory along the border. ASF ODAs are expected to each take 20 km^2 of enemy territory per month.
  - *Objective 3:* SOF trains the 1st AA battalion (BTN) to partner with ASF ODAs in service of COIN objectives along the Atropia-Ariana border. At least one battalion should be trained by August 2020.
- LOE 2: Precision targeting.
  - *Objective 1:* Degrade terrorist organizations that attacked the British and U.S. embassies and are preparing for further assaults. All terrorist activities around Baku must cease within three months.
  - *Objective 2:* Reduce budding support for Ariana among the more radicalized Shi'a elements of the Atropia population.
- LOE 3: Influence via MISO.
  - *Objective 1:* Decrease swelling population support for Ariana among more-isolated and tribal areas in southern Atropia. Pro-

vision of food, shelter, intelligence, and other resources to these forces should cease by August 2020.
  - *Objective 2:* Develop national pride and support for the expanding ASF. Provision of intelligence and material support for the ASF should increase (ideally, at least double) between March and August 2020.
- LOE 4: Influence via CAO.
  - *Objective 1:* Build local leadership structures and support for this local governance in the southern territories who are loyal to Atropia. Support for local governance should increase to at least 75 percent by August 2020 (over an estimated baseline measurement of 60 percent support in January 2020).
  - *Objective 2:* Degrade the shadow governments loyal to Ariana that have established themselves in the most war-torn southern Atropian territories. Support for shadow governments should decrease by at least 25 percent by August 2020 (over an estimated baseline measurement of 40 percent support in January 2020).

Note that all these objectives identify specific thresholds with expected dates of achievement. The assessment team engaged with the command to set these thresholds and to ensure that the commander believed they were achievable within the identified time horizon. This ensured that all objectives meet the SMART criteria.

Step 2. Identify Activities

Having determined a list of military objectives pertaining to each SOJTF-Atropia LOE, the next step for the assessment team was to read operational plans and consult with command staff to determine the U.S. special operations forces (USSOF) activities designed to achieve the objectives determined in Step 1. To do this, the assessment team first completed the five-W worksheet from Table 4.1. Specifically, the team answered who, what, where, when, and why questions for each LOE, including planned MOPs from the results of these questions. Box 5.1 illustrates the process for activities conducted for LOE 1 (develop, enable, and employ partner force). SOF planners have already determined that the ASF has no existing special forces and that special forces operations are required to clear and defeat forces loyal to Ariana.

After filling out this worksheet to plot the five-W and MOP dimensions of USSOF activities in support of LOE 1, the assessment team developed a set of mission tracker spreadsheets to record the aspects of SOF activities critical for assessment purposes. In this case, the theory of change, the why field, is fairly straightforward because LOE 1 involves clearance operations to take enemy territory. To structure data collection, the team developed separate mission tracker spreadsheets for (1) SOF recruitment and training of ASF and the 1st AA BTN and (2) partnered USSOF/ASF COIN operations.

As an example, the assessment team spreadsheet for SOF recruitment and training activities (for the ASF and 1st AA BTN) involved a monthly interval for data collection, while the spreadsheet for partnered COIN operations involved weekly data collection. Table 5.1 illustrates how each activity tracker spreadsheet was structured.

Box 5.1
SOJTF-Atropia Mission Tracker Worksheet, LOE 1

Activities: USSOF will conduct recruitment and training events to build the ASF, using a training headquarters near Baku. USSOF will also use this training headquarters to train the 1st AA BTN how to partner with the ASF. SOJTF-Atropia will coordinate ASF COIN activities in southern Atropia.

Who: Atropian Special Police Forces (ASPF) and other SAPA forces (enemy). ASF and 1st AA BTN (friendly).

What: Increased ASF manning and operational capabilities. 1st AA BTN shows ability to partner with ASF. ASPF and SAPA degraded in southern territories.

Where: USSOF ODAs will hold recruitment events throughout Atropia. Training of ASF and the 1st AA BTN will take place outside Baku. ASF COIN activities will take place in southern territories.

When: Recruitment will begin in March 2020, with training stating in April. First ASF COIN activities will commence in June 2020.

Why: USSOF recruitment and training will develop six elite ASF ODAs that are capable of partnering with both USSOF and Atropia Army units. Clearance operations (in coordination with USSOF) will create significant losses among ASPF on southern border.

MOP: Training and recruitment events, trained ASF and 1st AA BTN personnel and units, COIN operations and battlefield effects.

Table 5.1
SOJTF-Atropia Mission Tracker Spreadsheets, LOE 1

ASF and 1st AA Battalion Recruitment and Training	March	April	May	June	July
Recruitment events	5	2	3	4	7
ASF new recruits	20	12	5	6	28
ASF recruit dropout	10	2	3	2	14
ASF battlefield attrition	1	3	8	1	2
ASF ODAs trained	0	1	0	1	2
ASF ODAs equipped	1	1	0	1	1
1st AA battalion companies trained	1	1	1	1	1

USSOF- and ASF-Partnered COIN Operations	June 3–9	June 10–16	June 17–23	June 24–30
Clearance operations	2	10	3	4
Patrols	1	5	10	12
Enemy attrition	6	24	0	16
ASF attrition	0	1	0	1
Weapons seized or destroyed	20	0	14	56
Vehicles seized or destroyed	3	2	1	5
Territory gained or lost (km^2)	10	21	–5	–10

NOTE: See Box 4.3 for additional details regarding conversions of mapped territory to numerical data.

Step 3. Define MOEs

Having defined mission LOEs, their objectives, and a set of activities to accomplish the objectives, the assessment team's next task is to develop MOEs that will help measure progress toward military objectives. The assessment team began by consulting the list of generic SOF MOEs by LOE in Chapter Three, then used conversations with the command to ensure the LOEs fit with the local operational context and measure dynamics that fit with the command's CONOP.

MOEs follow from operational objectives and must measure progress toward the objectives. For the purposes of illustration, we will show how the objectives for LOE 2 (precision targeting) led to specific MOEs. The operational objectives for SOJTF-Atropia under LOE 2 are as follows:

- *Objective 1:* Degrade ASPF units that attacked the British and U.S. embassies and are preparing for further assaults.
- *Objective 2:* Reduce budding support for Ariana among more-radicalized Shi'a elements of the Atropia population.

The MOEs suggested in Chapter Three for precision targeting (see Table 3.2) include "enemy personnel and materiel losses." Assume that the assessment team has set up a mission tracker framework much like the one in the earlier example for partner-force activities (LOE 1). This mission tracker will include data on air strikes and ground assaults on known or suspected ASPF terrorist cells in and around Baku. Each precision targeting operation would also record enemy killed in action and records of enemy equipment and infrastructure destroyed. With this mission tracker data, the assessment team can convert Objective 1 into MOE 1 for precision targeting: *Enemy losses of personnel, equipment, and infrastructure linked with SOF unilateral air and ground assaults.* Consulting Chapter Three further, the assessment team notes "disruptions of enemy operations" as a recommended MOE for precision targeting. Consulting with the J2, the assessment team determines that sufficient intelligence assets are in place near Baku to capture this level of subtlety in enemy plans and activities. With the specific operational objectives for the Baku area in mind, the assessment team added MOE 2, *ASPF terrorist cells cancel or diminish plans for further attacks in and around Baku.*

Finally, the assessment team sees that "reduced population expressions of enemy support" is recommended as an MOE, as is measuring reductions in true (physical and materiel) support to the enemy. After consulting with the command, the assessment team learned that very sophisticated intelligence on population cooperation with the ASPF and other Ariana forces is available, but there is no evidence of direct population collusion with the ASPF in and around Baku. Thus, the assessment team developed three MOEs for the precision targeting LOE and two MOEs for Objective 1:

- *Objective 1:* Degrade ASPF units that attacked the British and U.S. embassies and are preparing for further assaults.
  - *MOE 1:* Enemy losses of personnel, equipment, and infrastructure linked with SOF unilateral air and ground assaults.
  - *MOE 2:* Cancelled or diminished ASPF terrorist cell plans for further attacks in and around Baku within three months of commencement of operations.

As described in Chapter Four, requirements for MOEs are that they be relevant, measurable, malleable, and distinct. The MOEs just established meet the relevance criterion because they are either explicitly or directly logically linked with the planned SOF activities. At first pass, they also meet the measurement criterion, with some data already available via the mission tracker and other data that the J2 has confirmed are available (in Step 4, "Develop Indicators and Collect Data"). Both MOEs assess dynamics that can be expected to change over months (or even weeks) in response to a powerful precision targeting campaign. Finally, the MOEs are distinct from each other, with MOE 1 assessing enemy losses and MOE 2 assessing changes in enemy behavior.

Step 4. Develop Indicators and Collect Data

With MOEs for all LOEs in place, the next task for the assessment team is to develop specific indicators for each MOE that are in turn supported by robust data streams that are feasible to collect. Here, we will illustrate how the assessment team arrived at a specific set of indicators and supporting data streams for LOE 3, "Influence via MISO." As illustrated in Step 1, the assessment team has identified the following objectives for SOJTF-Atropia's influence via MISO during Operation Western Peace. Let us also assume that the team has proceeded through Step 3 and has identified a set of associated MOEs:

- *Objective 1:* Decrease swelling population support for Ariana among more isolated, tribal areas in southern Atropia. Provision of food, shelter, intelligence and other resources to these forces should cease by August 2020.
  - *MOE 1:* Decreased population expressions of support for SAPA and ASPF between March and August 2020 (ideally approaching zero).
  - *MOE 2:* Decreased provision of safe harbor and information to ASPF in southern territories between March and August 2020 (ideally approaching zero).
- *Objective 2:* Develop national pride and support for the expanding ASF. Provision of intelligence and materiel support for the ASF should increase (ideally by at least double) between March and August 2020.
  - *MOE 3:* Increased expressions of nationalism, pride, and victory celebrations linked with ASF and ASF operations between March and August 2020 (ideally doubling or more).
  - *MOE 4:* Increased provision of safe harbor and intelligence to ASF along southern border between March and August 2020 (ideally doubling or more).

Note that the assessment team is ultimately interested in behavioral change but has included one cognitive change MOE in each case. With this list of MOEs in hand, the assessment team constructed a mission tracker for MISO activities, similar to one in Table 5.1 but focused on the location, media channel, and content of MISO efforts. The assessment team then consulted Chapter Three for recommendations about indicators and supporting data streams for these MOEs (see Table 3.3). This table suggested using traditional and social media as ambient data streams for measuring population support for the enemy (SAPA and ASPF) and against the ASF and Atropia more generally. It also suggested using polling data and interviews with the population as possible data sources for measuring population patterns of support. However, the assessment team decided that levels of conflict in the areas of highest interest (southern Atropia) were (1) too high to justify the risk to a data collection team and (2) likely to make local citizens so suspicious of data collectors that responses could be biased by low participation rates and/or deliberate falsification of responses (see Box 4.2 for a related discussion). Thus, while polling and interview data were potentially quite relevant, were malleable over time (at least theoretically), and could be aggregated appropriately in time and place, they would be subject to unknown and potentially high degrees of bias and would require a level of investment that is difficult to justify (see data stream inclusion and exclusion criteria, Figure 4.2).

Given these concerns with polling and interview data, the assessment team settled on using traditional and social media reports as data streams for MOE 1 and MOE 3. Since the onset of conflict along the border, traditional media coverage had shrunk significantly, leading to a fairly narrow data set of newspaper, radio, and television coverage that could be read and coded by a small team of Arabic speakers to indicate whether each media release was mostly positive, negative, or neutral regarding the forces and activities of Atropia and Ariana. Meanwhile, the volume of social media data was too large to hand-code using assessment team staff, so the team used an automated text-analysis tool to analyze sentiments (in Arabic) in social media posts geotagged as coming from Atropia. The team set a monthly interval for collecting and coding these data, resulting in a monthly data matrix (see Table 5.2).

To categorize traditional media coverage as positive, negative, and neutral, the team started by conducting open thematic analysis of media content from TV channels, radio stations, and newspapers.[3] While the initial coding scheme was more extensive, the team realized during discussions that—likely due to the polarizing effects of war and both adversaries' direct influence on the media—most content had a clear narrative agenda of characterizing either Atropia or Ariana in a positive or negative light. Meanwhile, a few dedicated independent channels did their best to show both sides of the conflict. Categorizing

[3] In the Atropia versus Ariana case, both segments of the population used TV, radio, newspaper, and social media quite regularly—with a slight bias for more social media use among younger demographic sectors. In certain areas of the world (e.g., Syria or Afghanistan), social media use is quite uncommon, and most news may travel by radio, text message, or even word of mouth.

Table 5.2
Monthly Media Reports Spreadsheet—Influence via MISO, LOE 3

	Positive	Neutral	Negative
Toward Atropia			
TV	25	2	3
Radio	18	7	4
Newspaper	30	3	10
Facebook	80	2	20
Twitter	924	5	325
Toward Ariana			
TV	5	1	20
Radio	6	3	14
Newspaper	2	5	17
Facebook	7	1	70
Twitter	414	3	1,012

social media content was more straightforward and relied on preexisting dictionaries indexing words and phrases associated with positive or negative sentiment.

As part of discussions with other staff while developing the MOEs, the assessment team confirmed with the J2 that intelligence assets were able to pick up chatter about the degree of control and collaboration the enemy was receiving from the local population. The team worked with the J2 to receive monthly reports of this chatter, including discrete counts of chatter mentioning provision of intelligence or safe harbor and counts of messages expressing frustration with decreased population compliance with the ASPF and Atropian forces.

The assessment team also consulted with ASF tactical units doing COIN operations along the southern border and developed a matrix to collect data on population collaboration with the ASF. Thus, data streams from the J2 regarding population support to the enemy and data streams from ASF ODAs on population support were both channeled into a monthly data matrix (see Table 5.3).

Table 5.3
Population Direct Support, to Enemy or Friendly, Spreadsheet—Influence via MISO, LOE 3

	March	April	May	June	July
Toward Atropia (from J2 Intel)					
Intelligence (tips, etc.)	1	5	7	21	45
Safe harbor (for people, weapons)	0	0	2	3	5
Direct materiel support (money, food, etc.)	1	2	6	2	8
Recruits (informal or formal manpower)	0	1	3	2	5
Reports of frustration (decreased support)	3	1	0	0	0
Toward Ariana (from ASF ODA SITREPs)					
Intelligence (tips, etc.)	3	2	0	0	0
Safe harbor (for people, weapons)	2	1	0	0	2
Direct materiel support (money, food, etc.)	4	2	1	0	3
Recruits (informal or formal manpower)	8	5	2	0	1
Reports of frustration (decreased support)	0	1	2	5	2

Step 5. Conduct Analysis

After developing objectives for each LOE (Step 1), identifying activities and setting up activity trackers (Step 2), and identifying MOEs (Step 3) and indicators and data streams for each MOE (Step 4), the next step for the assessment team is to select the appropriate analytic methods and run analysis. We will illustrate using the data analysis step for the influence via CAO LOE for SOJTF-Atropia (LOE 4), showing how thresholds from objectives were integrated into the MOEs that the assessment team developed.

Assume that the assessment team has proceeded through Steps 1–4 for the CAO LOE, resulting in the following objectives and MOEs:

- *LOE 4: Influence via CAO.* SOF will conduct unilateral and partnered CAO—in coordination with USAID and other development agencies if feasible—focused in the southern territories.
  - *Objective 1:* Build local leadership structures and support for this local governance in the southern territories that are loyal to Atropia.
    - *MOE 1*: Increased Atropian population expressions of support for ASF-backed local government entities in southern Atropia. Support for local governance should increase to at least 75 percent by August 2020 (over an estimated baseline measurement of 60 percent in January 2020).
    - *MOE 2:* Evidence of increased southern Atropian participation in local government elections and civic events by at least 25 percent between March and August 2020.
    - *MOE 3:* Evidence of increased economic activity following repair from the devastation caused by Ariana forces and liberation from their extreme restrictions on population movement by at least 25 percent in next three months.
  - *Objective 2:* Degrade the shadow governments loyal to Ariana that have established themselves in the most war-torn southern Atropia territories.
    - *MOE 4:* Decreased Atropian population expressions for shadow governance established by insurgents loyal to Ariana. Support for shadow government should decrease by at least 25 percent by August 2020 (over an estimated baseline measurement of 40 percent in January 2020).
    - *MOE 5:* Decreased population cooperation with insurgent governance forces loyal to Ariana between March and August 2020 (ideally converging on zero).

During Step 2, the assessment team established an activity tracker for CAO in southern Atropia identifying numbers of certain types of CAO per month, monthly numbers of southern Atropia citizens participating in events, and the total amount of money spent on development projects per month (see Table 5.4)

Furthermore, during Step 4 the assessment team reviewed possible indicators and supporting data stream for the effects of CA, using guidance from Chapter Three (see Table 3.4). As discussed earlier under Step 4 (data and indicators), the assessment team decided against collecting polling and interview data from the southern Atropia population at this point, given concerns about safety and cost and about the potentially extreme bias data collection might introduce in an area with such high levels of ongoing turmoil.

The team was able to leverage its data collection of traditional and social media channels for assessment of LOE 3 (Influence via MISO) to also code for positive and negative sentiments toward the local ASF-

Table 5.4
SOJTF-Atropia Mission Tracker—Influence via CAO to Support Friendly Entity, LOE 4

CAO Activities	March	April	May	June	July	August
Local governor elections	5	3	2	0	3	5
Key leader engagements	14	20	40	12	0	0
Local hiring events	0	3	10	15	10	8
Development projects—educational	0	2	4	10	12	14
Development projects—medical	10	8	7	6	3	10
Development projects—economic	0	0	0	3	6	20
Development projects—religious	5	3	2	0	0	0
Development projects—security	0	4	7	10	14	27
Development projects—total $000 spent	39	44	80	156	224	193
Count of unique residents attending or participating in events or projects	230	836	1,022	750	300	395

backed governance and for positive and negative sentiments toward the insurgent shadow governments loyal to Ariana. The team used the monthly traditional and social media reports to produce a month-by-month measure of sentiment (positive minus negative reports) for both ASF-backed and insurgent-backed governing entities (see Table 5.5).

Similar to Table 5.2, the assessment team was also able to channel ASF ODA SITREPs and intelligence from J2 into a table of population direct assistance and participation or cooperation with ASF-backed local governance, as opposed to cooperation with the shadow insurgent governance loyal to Ariana. Finally, the team leveraged another ambient data stream—satellite data showing electrical coverage and agricultural production over time.

With data for only six months and a wide variety of data streams for this LOE, the assessment team started by visualizing the data in simple Excel line and bar charts, complemented by correlations between "input" (mission tracker) and "output" effects data, such as traditional and social media positive versus negative reports, satellite data, and cooperation with ASF-backed versus insurgent-backed governance. For example, the assessment team looked at trajectories of media support over time, using the data in Table 5.5 (with social media numbers scaled down by a factor of 10 to allow for comparison of traditional and social media).

Table 5.5
Monthly Sentiment Toward Friendly and Enemy Entities—Influence via CAO, LOE 4

Positive-Negative Sentiment Reports	March	April	May	June	July	August
Traditional media (combined) reports on ASF-backed governance	–10	–5	5	20	30	50
Social media (combined) posts on ASF-backed governance	–77	–50	–90	125	–229	75
Traditional media (combined) reports on shadow governance	0	–5	–10	0	–29	–69
Social media (combined) posts on shadow governance	107	88	525	350	877	1,024

Through simple data visualization (see Figure 5.1), the team noticed several patterns. Traditional media demonstrated an upward trend in support for ASF-backed local governance and a drop in support for insurgent-backed governance. Given the thresholds from the objectives for LOE 4, these changes were determined to be meaningful. However, the trends in social media sentiment were different: Support for ASF-governance fell dramatically between June and July, while support for the insurgent-backed governance began to trend upward. Confused by these results and unable to find any clear "drivers" of this pattern among the bivariate correlations that it ran, the assessment team went back to SITREP reports and to specific tweets and Facebook posts from the June–July time frame. The team discovered that effects from another LOE—precision targeting—were likely responsible for the patterns the team saw. In particular, two high-profile civilian casualty (CIVCAS) events related to precision drone strikes occurred in this time frame (see dotted lines in Figure 5.1), and the Ariana social media campaign took explicit advantage of these

Figure 5.1
Monthly Trajectory of Media Sentiment—Influence via CAO (LOE 4)

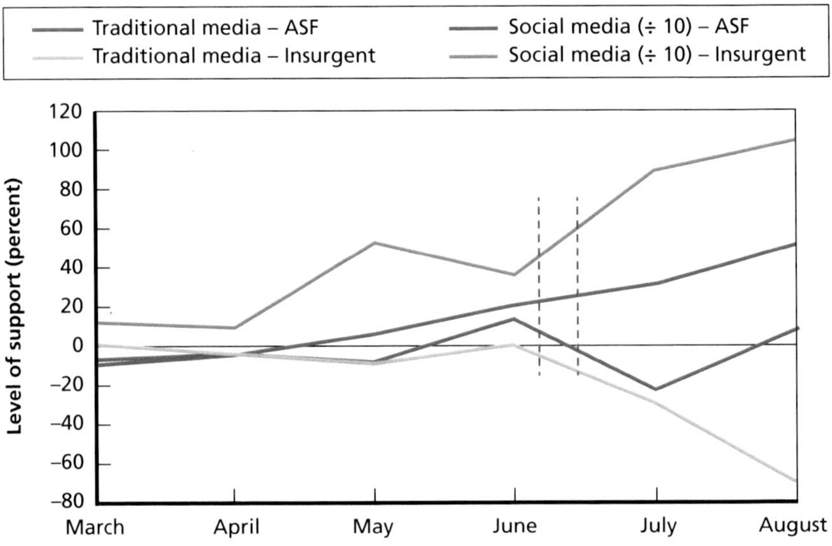

events, using what appeared to be bots and other amplifiers on social media to exploit these events in Ariana's favor.

Step 6: Consolidate Analysis

Through a series of parallel data visualization and analysis steps, the assessment team put together an introductory slide featuring an LOE-specific quad chart for the commander summarizing main findings for each LOE, with back-up slides to provide additional details on analytic process and trends over time as needed. See Figure 5.2 for the quad chart for the commander, which presents the bottom line up front. The assessment team has indicated, for each LOE, where warning thresholds have been met or surpassed as areas of potential concern to the commander (i.e., possibly requiring challenging the CONOP or requiring adjustment to operations) in bold type for each LOE. For example, with three ASF ODAs operating for three months, the mission tracker warning threshold was set for each ASF ODA to gain 20 km^2 of territory per month. With only 27 km^2 of total territorial gain, this warning threshold has been met and surpassed. For LOEs with specific regional considerations—the core area of territorial gain and loss for LOE 1 (partner forces), the area of radical Shi'a support for Atropia relevant to LOE 2 (precision targeting), and the location of the CIVCAS incident affecting LOE 4 (CAO)—the team has indicated the area or location of concern with red arrows pointing to a map of the Atropia area of operations.

Additional slides in the briefing provided further details, including a summary of interactions (both expected and newly detected) among LOEs. For example, the assessment team highlighted that the original CONOP presumed that the effects of precision targeting and PYSOP activity would mutually reinforce each other. That is, precision strikes against ASPF, coupled with coverage of these strikes on social media and other channels, would help consolidate resistance to Ariana and loyalty to Atropia. However, the team noted that CIVCAS from precision strikes allowed the enemy to reverse the rise of populist loyalty to Atropia shown earlier in the campaign.

Figure 5.2
Introductory Assessment Slide, SOJTF-Atropia 2020 March–August

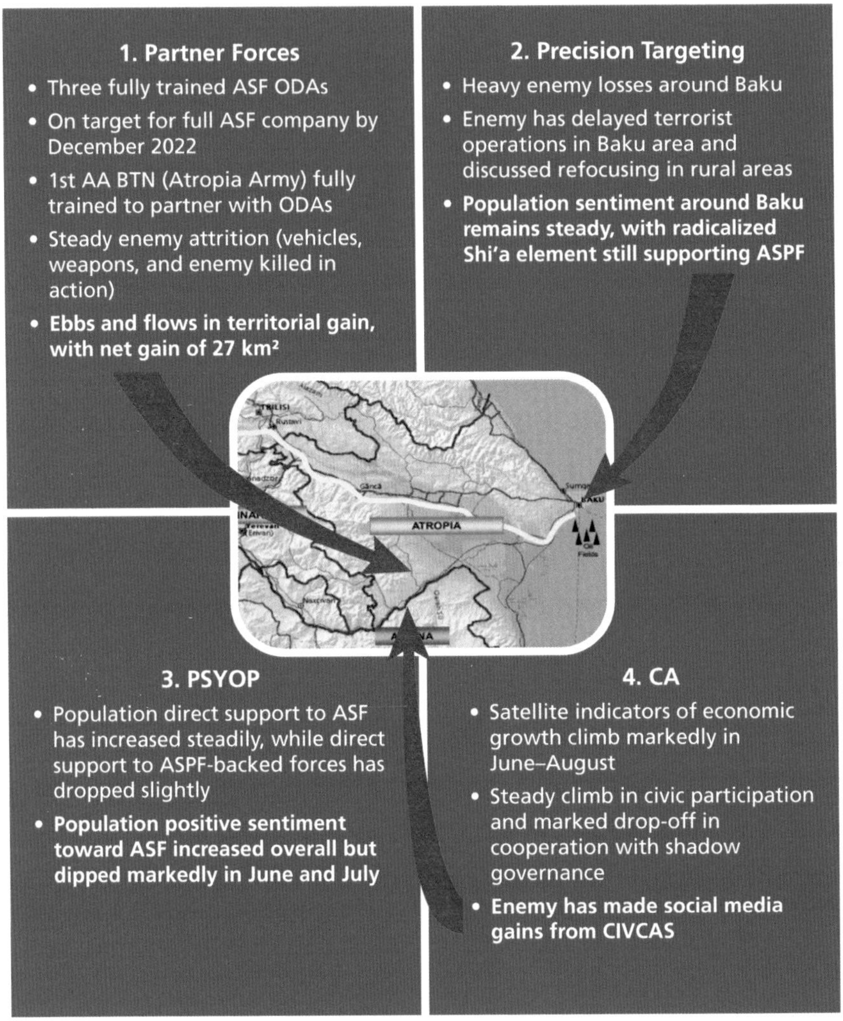

Step 7: Review

During the briefing, the commander decided to review and propose a revision of rules of engagement for precision strikes in high population

density areas. He also asked the assessment team to conduct a more detailed review of ASF ODA SITREPs and other operational reporting to determine why some partnered operations were linked with territorial gains and others with losses and to coordinate with ASF ODA trainers to develop a plan to address any capability gaps leading to losses. Both commander actions were inspired by the assessment team's noting that specific thresholds linked with objectives had not been achieved over the prior three months of operations.

After conducting its post-briefing review, the assessment team decided to make two modifications to its assessment process for the next assessment period. First, the team set up monthly check-ins to determine whether any data trends that were formerly moving in the desired directions had changed course. In these cases, the assessment team would speak with command staff and explore SITREPs to try to determine a cause for these changes. Second, the team decided to add topical analysis to the list of outputs for monthly social media reports to help the team notice emerging trends, such as the enemy use of the recent CIVCAS event, and inform PSYOP personnel in a timelier manner. Overall, the assessment team noted that it had influenced command decisionmaking because the commander had changed some rules of engagement to avoid the damaging effects of future CIVCAS incidents.

CHAPTER SIX

Final Considerations

In this final chapter, we outline some final considerations for operational-level assessments of special operations efforts. The first section discusses recommended practices for refining the collection and structuring of operational data to enable the most efficient exploitation for assessment purposes. The second discusses emerging technologies—both in terms of available data and analytical methods—and how they may or may not be useful for SOF assessment. The final section describes the unique value that structured tactical-level reporting—including both SITREPs and intelligence reporting—can have for improving assessment efforts.

Preparing Operational Data for Assessment

Using operational data—the data that the operational-level headquarters and its subordinate elements *already* produce—is critical for our assessment approach. These are highly granular data on the types of activities that the operational-level headquarters is involved in and provide a unique perspective on environmental factors that can function as indicators for many SOF MOEs. In this section, we first describe how the tactical-level SITREP can be standardized to support assessment and then outline the types of additional data that the operational-level headquarters itself should collate. *Importantly, none of the data enumerated in this section should entail additional collection, at either the tactical or operational level, beyond what is already required to support existing operational requirements.*

The tactical-level SITREP "enhances the unit's understanding of their local environment and facilitates their ability to organize the fight and more effectively manage that environment,"[1] so it contains an enormous amount of information about the operations the tactical-level element conducts and about the atmospherics of the operational environment. While SITREPs are a powerful tool for providing situational awareness to higher-level headquarters, they are rarely analyzed systematically and longitudinally, in part because much of the key information is provided only as narratives.[2] To exploit the richness of data available in these SITREPs, our assessment approach proposes a standardized SITREP that can be readily collated across time and units to provide data for assessment.[3]

The standardized weekly SITREP that we propose, summarized in Table 6.1, would have three key components. The first would be a summary of the key events for the week—namely, all activities that might influence any of the LOEs and associated objectives. They key events would be organized by LOE and include a one-paragraph syn-

---

1 Joint Warfighting Center, 2011, p. G-10.

2 An additional concern is that, because such SITREPs often contain sensitive personnel information, they are not available beyond the immediate headquarters for a given tactical-level element. For a discussion of the difficulty that this narrative format presents for analysis of SITREPs, see Nicholas Rabinowitz, "The OCHA Sitrep: Open Access and Political Pressure in Humanitarian Information," master's thesis, Berkeley, Calif.: University of California, Berkeley, 2009, and Shannon Worthan, "Assessing the Impact of Information Channels on the Understanding of Ground Truth," master's thesis, Monterey, Calif.: Naval Postgraduate School, 2012. While there are automated tools for parsing narrative data, these analytic approaches are not yet advanced enough to automatically deliver the important elements of summarized information and nuanced meaning (see, e.g., Ying Zhao, Douglas J. MacKinnon, and Shelley P. Gallup, "System Self-Awareness and Related Methods for Improving the Use and Understanding of Data Within DoD," *Software Quality Professional*, Vol. 13, No. 4, September 2011; Li Zheng, Chao Shen, Liang Tang, Chunqiu Zeng, Tao Li, Steve Luis, Shu-Ching Chen, and Jainendra K. Navlakha, "Disaster SITREP—A Vertical Search Engine and Information Analysis Tool in Disaster Management Domain," presented at the 2012 IEEE 13th International Conference on Information Reuse and Integration (IRI), August 8–10, 2012).

3 Ninette Kelley, Peta Sandison, and Simon Lawry-White, *Enhancing UNHCR's Capacity to Monitor the Protection, Rights and Well-Being of Refugees*, Geneva: United Nations High Commissioner for Refugees Evaluation and Policy Analysis Unit, EPAU/2004/06, June 2004, used a similar approach.

Table 6.1
Key Elements of a Standardized Weekly Situation Report for Tactical Units

Category	Types of information
Key events	Synopsis and 5 Ws for all events likely to significantly affect at least one LOE. Include partner-force events (if known and applicable).
LOE-specific atmospherics	Summary of intelligence and atmospherics related to any of the LOEs (attitude of population, enemy morale, etc.)
Assessment of the sphere of influence	Geographic product describing the sphere of influence of the SOF element, partner force (if applicable), and enemy (if known and applicable).

opsis and the 5 Ws for the event—this would include operations conducted by partners, if that information is available. The second component would be a short (three to four sentences), weekly summary of changes in the operating environment, characterizing them as moving toward or away from the directions defined in the LOEs. The third component would be a qualitative evaluation of the sphere of influence of the tactical element.

The second class of operational data includes a myriad of information that staff sections in operational-level SOF headquarters already collect. Table 6.2 lists the types of information each staff section should collect.[4] These information requirements can be summarized as follows: J1 (manpower), SOF personnel and their geographic distribution; J2 (intelligence), enemy-, population-, and partner-focused intelligence; J3 (operations), mission and CONOP trackers; J4 (logistics), materiel provided to partners; J7 (partnering), partner-focused operational data; and J9 (civil-military operations), CA-focused operational data. J6 (communications) would take responsibility for maintaining a single location on the command's portal with pages for each staff section. This portal should be updated weekly, with a graphical dashboard interface to allow the commander and command staff to view all critical functions and status.

---

[4] The information to be collected both tracks SOF activities (Step 2 in our assessment approach) and provides indicators for selected MOEs (Step 4).

Table 6.2
Headquarters Information Requirements for Operational-Level Assessment

Staff Section	Types of data
J1 (Manpower)	• **SOF personnel statistics:** Manning levels, geographic distribution of tactical elements
J2 (Intelligence)	• **Enemy-focused intelligence:** Summaries of known enemy operations, territorial control, attrition, recruitment, morale • **Population-focused intelligence:** Summaries of pattern of life (e.g., economic activity, functioning of local government) and population attitude toward and engagement with enemy, partner forces, and SOF • **Partner force–focused intelligence (if available):** Partner morale, operational effectiveness
J3 (Operations)	• **CONOP tracker:** Filed, approved (at each required level), requests for support, ultimate disposition • **Mission tracker:** Roll-up of inputs from subordinate elements, ISR missions, kinetic strikes
J39 (Information Operations)	• : Aligned with CONOPs, location, specific activity, manning, strategic engagement, perceived outcomes
J4 (Logistics)	• **Materiel:** Requests and delivery schedule for equipment provided to partners, especially Class I (food), II (clothing and equipment), V (ammunition), VIII (medical), IX (repair parts)
J7 (Training and Development)	• **Partner force:** – *Manpower:* Recruitment, manning levels, causalities, key demographics – *Training:* Number and type of trained personnel – *Equipping:* Received, on hand, operable – *Operations:* Location, complexity • **Irregulars:** – *Manpower:* Vetting process, enrolled, trained, equipped – *Operations:* Location, complexity, relationship to official entities
J9 (Civil-Military Operations)	• **CA activities:** Aligned with CONOPs, location, specific activity, manning, strategic engagement, perceived outcomes

NOTE: These information requirements support both Step 2 and Step 4 of the assessment process. The commander, chief of staff, and J3 are critical to ensure that data is collected and delivered to the assessment team, and that a collaborative process is developed.

One of the persistent challenges of using operational data involves the danger of self-report bias, whether at the tactical (ODA), operational (SOJTF), or strategic level. The process of sorting, selecting,

and framing SITREPs as they are consolidated and reported up the chain leads to selective data loss; in some cases, this may exclude critical observations about activities that are not producing the expected effects. Adding structure to the SITREP and operational reporting process can help mitigate some of this self-report bias. Triangulation among observers is also critical for overcoming bias; for example, a company commander can provide some oversight and fact-checking on individual tactical reports from ODAs.

Emerging Data Streams—Potential and Limits of Social Media

Due to new technological capabilities to generate, store, and share data, the world now produces more data each year than can feasibly be analyzed—even with rapidly advancing computational approaches for making sense of large quantities of unstructured data (see the next section). This growth in available data is expected to continue increasing exponentially.[5] While fewer data are available in the denied and developing areas in which SOF often operates, the penetration of mobile technology into every corner of the world means that these areas are often still quite rich in personally generated data. Whether these individuals fully realize it or not, this creates new data sources that can be exploited for the purposes of SOF operational assessment.

The largest of these data sources is loosely categorized as *social media*. As described in the next section, new computational approaches to making sense out of largely unstructured textual, image, and even audio and video content on social media are quickly bringing much of social media "big data" into view. The commercial world has been quick to jump on these opportunities, with new social media analytics platforms entering the public sphere at a rapid pace. However, despite the proliferation of new ways to ingest, visualize, and analyze social media data, it is important to keep several caveats in mind.

---

[5] James M. Tien, "Big Data: Unleashing Information," *Journal of Systems Science and Systems Engineering*, Vol. 22, No. 2, June 1, 2013.

The first is by now a familiar problem: Unlike the early years of social media expansion, data are becoming increasingly hard to come by. More than 50 percent of Facebook pages are now private, accessible only to internal Facebook corporate researchers.[6] Some countries, such as China, maintain their own proprietary data sets of social media content. And many social media platforms, including Twitter, are making their aggregated data more difficult to come by. These individual, corporate, and country-level data restrictions exacerbate an already troublesome sampling bias issue with social media. For example, only 20 percent of the world uses the most popular open platform, Twitter, and every platform has a unique demographic profile that is not representative of the population as a whole.[7] These trends in the evolving social media landscape mean that assessment teams will need to become more creative in accessing various types of ambient data, while respecting privacy protections and applicable laws and regulations.

Additional inferential challenges plague analysis of social media for assessing operations. For example, each platform provides a specific mechanism for interaction and, therefore, a limited window on the wider sphere of human interaction. Focusing only on social media could easily lead to the conclusion that social media was *the* driver of the Arab Spring. However, a deeper analysis reveals that network news, carefully curated websites, text messaging, and face-to-face interaction (as well as the initiation of the revolution in Tunisia) were just as critical (if not more so) in the spread of Arab revolutionary events.[8] Furthermore, social media can easily be dominated by outsized power users, some of whom may be automated bots employed by foreign governments or other non-U.S. interests. Without accounting for these influences, analysts risk having their analyses manipulated by potential

---

6 Zeynep Tufekci, "Big Questions for Social Media Big Data: Representativeness, Validity and Other Methodological Pitfalls," *Proceedings of the Eighth International AAAI Conference on Weblogs and Social Media*, 2014.

7 Tufekci, 2014.

8 Zeynep Tufekci and Christopher Wilson, "Social Media and the Decision to Participate in Political Protest: Observations from Tahrir Square," *Journal of Communication*, Vol. 62, No. 2, 2012.

adversaries.[9] Social media are also explicitly a public presentation of the self, so individual users heavily filter the information they present to the outside world.[10]

Despite these challenges, social media have many unique advantages for SOF operational analysis. With the spread of mobile devices across the globe, social media often open a unique window on activist, political, insurgent, and other movements as they emerge and spread. Social media platforms are one of the most common tools movements use as they mobilize and organize and so can give excellent early warning of networks coalescing into political or activist groups. Furthermore, more-open social media platforms, such as Twitter, are explicitly *conversational*; that is, they capture real-world interactions between multiple groups and can lay bare key grievances, styles of communication, and points of potential agreement or collaboration among organized groups or different demographic sectors.[11] To the extent that social media platforms are emotional outlets and platforms for sharing strong sentiment, they can also be useful indicators of population or group sentiment about the effects of ongoing conflict and the impact of death, disease, and displacement—as well as who is to blame for these effects and where the population's loyalty is tilting.

Emerging Technologies—Making Sense of Unstructured Data

A suite of new developments in computational analysis promises to affect SOF assessment practices. The first—and most widely used—of

---

[9] Samuel C. Woolley, "Automating Power: Social Bot Interference in Global Politics," *First Monday*, Vol. 21, No. 4, April 2016.

[10] Eileen Y. L. Ong, Y. L., Rebecca P. Ang, Jim C. M. Ho, Joylynn C. Y. Lim, Dion H. Goh, Chei Sian Lee, and Alton Y. K. Chua, "Narcissism, Extraversion and Adolescents' Self-Presentation on Facebook," *Personality and Individual Differences*, Vol. 50, No. 2, January 2011.

[11] However, Tufekci, 2014, pp. 510–512, offers analytic caveats and discusses complexities in conversational mechanisms (such as subtweets) that may be missed by traditional machine-based analytic approaches.

these is text analysis. Computational text analysis allows the user to analyze more text than human beings can usefully read. Computers can be used in fully automated ways to read mass quantities of text for a human analyst and provide prestructured results. Computers can also be used as an analytic prosthetic, showing the analyst where to look for likely needles in the haystacks of text data. Text analytics falls roughly into the following categories:

- **Document clustering and querying** is a machine-learning approach that sorts large document collections (tens of thousands of documents or more) into smaller clusters of related documents, then uses smart querying to extract relevant information, e.g., "Find me the documents about *Russia* operating in *Syria*."
- **Human-supervised text classification** involves teaching a machine to classify text by learning from human examples. For example, a human might code 1,000 tweets for operationally relevant categories; the machine learns from that example, then codes 500,000 tweets.
- **Topic modeling** is a method of extracting the topics in very large text collections (millions of words), including comparative analysis.
- **Lexical analysis** is a word-based technique for extracting keywords and abstractions (place names, proper names, and abstract concepts).
- **Sentiment analysis** is a process for categorizing opinions expressed in a piece of text to determine whether the text expresses an attitude is positive, negative, or neutral toward a topic.
- **Stance analysis** is a more powerful version of sentiment analysis that extracts personal and sociocultural information, such as affect, social relationships, values, confidence, person categories (i.e., first person versus third person), narrative style, and temporality (the tendency to refer to the past, present, or future).

In examining social media data sets, text analysis can be combined with social network analysis to examine how communities that

interact with each other show distinct linguistic signatures.[12] New developments in resonance analysis use statistical techniques to model the spread of specific linguistic signatures through networks and can be used to gauge the impact of MISO or enemy propaganda.[13]

As they become more sophisticated and user-friendly, text analytic approaches will change the face of open-source intelligence analysis, allowing much more rapid analysis of massive amounts of data.[14] Additionally, a large percentage of military operational data (e.g., SITREPs) comes in the form of semistructured or unstructured text and is therefore amenable to computational text analysis. Text analysis has the ability to dramatically shorten the time and energy required to hand-code SITREPs, interview transcripts, articles, and other long-form textual output for assessment purposes.

Additionally, nontextual data are now amenable to machine-learning and artificial intelligence approaches for classification and analysis. Automated image analysis has made rapid strides,[15] including the ability to classify aerial images similar to those of ISR captures.[16] Meanwhile, new developments in automated processing of media (audio and video) content allow classification, indexing, and analysis

---

[12] Elizabeth Bodine-Baron, Todd C. Helmus, Madeline Magnuson, and Zev Winkelman, *Examining ISIS Support and Opposition Networks on Twitter*, Santa Monica, Calif.: RAND Corporation, RR-1328-RC, 2016

[13] As an example, Bodine-Baron et al., 2016, collected official social media posts from both ISIS and the Muslim Brotherhood to construct digital thumbprints for each group. These thumbprints were then compared against some 6 million tweets from across Egypt to identify whether the number of supporters of each changed over time. (The researchers found that support for ISIS increased, but support for the Muslim Brotherhood decreased.)

[14] A cautionary note for open-source analysis is that written text samples are rarely representative of the population at large; this goes both for formal writing and for more "democratized" platforms, such as social media.

[15] Alexander Krizhevsky, Ilya Sutskever, and Geoffrey E. Hinton, "System and Method for Generating Training Cases for Image Classification," U.S. Patent, February 2, 2016.

[16] Adriana Romero, Carlo Gatta, and Gustau Camps-Valls, "Unsupervised Deep Feature Extraction for Remote Sensing Image Classification," *IEEE Transactions on Geoscience and Remote Sensing*, Vol. 54, No. 3, 2016.

of this online content as well.[17] While analytic tools for images, audio, and video are in their infancy, this promises to open up an additional treasure trove of data and insights into the cognitive states, emotions, and communication of SOF enemies and host-nation populations.

Steady-State and Preventive Operations

Many SOF operations have been noncombat missions conducted to prevent instability—i.e., in El Salvador, SOF maintained a training and advisory mission to support El Salvador's counterinsurgency from 1981–1992[18]—or have focused on preventing instability.[19] This remains the case today with SOF operating in the U.S. Southern Command region focused on long-duration capacity building of partners and COIN, while those in the U.S. Africa Command region focused, at least to some extent, on conflict prevention. Named operations with counterterrorism objectives are part of the special operations' activities in Africa, but the majority of activities are noncombat missions that occur under peacetime authorities, rather than execute or operational orders that authorize combat. Such activities occur at the discretion of the ambassador. Thus, incorporation of reporting on interagency efforts and priorities is critical in the assessment of steady-state operations. Additionally, these steady-state operations involve long-term understand and influence missions.

These steady-state operations create unique challenges for assessment. For steady-state missions, meaningful changes in the MOEs should only be detectable over similarly long periods. This makes causal inference particularly difficult because the operating environment is also anticipated to change in many other ways during extended time frames. For conflict prevention missions, it is much more difficult

17 Ryan Steelberg and Chad Steelberg, "Engine and System for the Transcription and Assessment of Media Files," U.S. Patent Application Publication, February 23, 2017.

18 Victor M. Rosello, "Lessons from El Salvador," *Parameters*, Vol. 23, Winter 1993–1994.

19 Henry H. Shelton, "Special Operations Forces: Key Role in Preventive Defense," *DISAM Journal*, 1997.

to prove that SOF presence and actions have prevented instability than it is to provide evidence of progress against a known enemy. Assessments of deterrence efforts face a similar challenge.[20]

Assessments of these types of SOF operations—which are also typically more limited in scope—will require an adapted version of the assessment approach detailed in this report. Specifically, while the MOEs and indicators will be analogous, the timeline for the analysis—which will likely need to be measured in years, not three-month blocks—and the types of analytical approaches will differ as well. For these types of operations, an assessment approach modeled after those used by development and law enforcement professionals is likely to be the most appropriate.[21] These approaches are optimized to account for the variety of confounding factors that influence the causal interpretation of analysis and rely on triangulation of both qualitative and quantitative methodologies. An additional consideration is that some of the principal activities in these theaters may be purely preparatory, and thus cannot be assessed in terms of achieving their ultimate objectives. Intermediate objectives, such as the degree to which access, knowledge, and placement have been achieved, must be measured against a defined and defensible benchmark of sufficiency.

Conclusion

For this assessment framework to be adopted by the SOF community, it will be necessary for commanders to issue guidance and for relevant changes to be implemented across the doctrine, organization, training, material, leadership development and education, personnel, and facilities spectrum.[22] Standardizing a process for assessments will require

[20] James Fearon, "Selection Effects and Deterrence," *International Interactions*, Vol. 28, No. 1, 2002.

[21] For example, World Bank, *Results Framework and M&E Guidance Note*, April 9, 2013. Also see United Nations Office on Drugs and Crime, "Criminal Justice Assessment Toolkit," webpage, 2006.

[22] See Joint Staff, 2011, pp. VI-1–VI-3.

several steps. Some version of this guide should be produced as a handbook for the force, and the main principles and practices of assessment should be incorporated into SOF doctrine. Assessment methods and appreciation of the vital importance of assessments as a commander's tool should be incorporated into professional military education, precommand courses, and premission training. In the field, assessments should become a more prominent facet of SOF commands' practice and should be incorporated into the commander's planning process and decisionmaking cycle. Assessment methods courses should be offered at the schoolhouses, and a SOF operational assessment course should be taught at the Joint Special Operations University to ensure dissemination to and adoption by joint SOF. Personnel and organizational implications include the need to assign sufficient numbers of trained personnel to the assessment cell, as part of the J5 of deployed operational headquarters staff. Finally, implementation will require appropriate facilities and materiel solutions, including access to the appropriate data streams and analytic platforms, and agreements for reachback support and data storage at relevant headquarters. In sum, to inculcate a culture of rigorous and dispassionate assessment, SOF leadership will have to embrace a comprehensive set of measures, such as those outlined here, from incorporation into doctrine to organizational change to training and education to the ultimate goal of routine implementation in the field.

Abbreviations

AA	Atropian Army
ADRP	Army doctrine reference publication
ALP	Afghan Local Police
ARSOF	Army Special Operations Forces
ASF	Atropian Special Forces
ASPF	Atropian Special Police Forces
ATP	Army techniques publication
BTN	battalion
CA	civil affairs
CAO	civil affairs operations
CAS	close air support
CERP	Commander's Emergency Response Program
CIVCAS	Civilian casualty
COIN	counterinsurgency
CONOP	concept of operation
FM	field manual
HUMINT	human intelligence

ISR	intelligence, surveillance, and reconnaissance
J1	Manpower
J2	Intelligence
J3	Operations
J39	Information Operations
J4	Logistics
J6	Communications
J7	Training and Development
J9	Civil-Military Operations
JDN	joint doctrine note
JP	joint publication
LOE	line of effort
MISO	military information support operations
MOE	measure of effectiveness
MOP	measure of performance
ODA	Operational Detachment Alpha
PSYOP	psychological operations
SAPA	South Atropian People's Party
SIGINT	signals intelligence
SITREP	situation report
SMART	specific, measurable, achievable, relevant, and time bound
SOF	special operations forces
SOJTF	Special Operations Joint Task Force

USAID	U.S. Agency for International Development
USASOC	U.S. Army Special Operations Command
USSOF	U.S. special operations forces
VSO	village stability operations
WMD	weapons of mass destruction

References

ADRP—*See* Army Doctrine Reference Publication.

Army Doctrine Reference Publication 5-0, *The Operations Process*, Washington, D.C.: Headquarters Department of the Army, 2012.

Army Techniques Publication 3-55.4, *Techniques for Information Collection During Operations Among Populations*, Washington, D.C.: Headquarters, Department of the Army, April 2016.

Army Techniques Publication 5-0.3, Marine Corps Reference Publication 5-1C, Navy Tactics, Techniques, and Procedures 5-01.3, Air Force Tactics, Techniques, and Procedures (AFTTP) 3-2.87, *Operation Assessment: Multi-Service Tactics, Techniques, and Procedures for Operation Assessment*, Air Land Sea Application (ALSA) Center, August 2015.

ATP—*See* Army Techniques Publication.

Babyak, Michael A., "What You See May Not Be What You Get: A Brief, Nontechnical Introduction to Overfitting in Regression-Type Models," *Psychosomatic Medicine*, Vol. 66, No. 3, 2004, pp. 411–421. As of September 21, 2017:
http://journals.lww.com/psychosomaticmedicine/Fulltext/2004/05000/What_You_See_May_Not_Be_What_You_Get__A_Brief.21.aspx

Baker, Ralph O., "The Decisive Weapon: A Brigade Combat Team Commander's Perspective on Information Operations," *Military Review*, May–June 2006, pp. 13–32.

Blanken, Leo J., and Jason J. Lepore, "Principals, Agents, and Assessment," in Leo J. Blanken, Hy Rothstein, and Jason J. Lepore, eds., *Assessing War: The Challenge of Measuring Success and Failure*, Washington, D.C.: Georgetown University Press, 2015.

Bodine-Baron, Elizabeth, Todd C. Helmus, Madeline Magnuson, and Zev Winkelman, *Examining ISIS Support and Opposition Networks on Twitter*, Santa Monica, Calif.: RAND Corporation, RR-1328-RC, 2016. As of September 22, 2017:
https://www.rand.org/pubs/research_reports/RR1328.html

Borgo, Rita, Johannes Kehrer, David Chung, Eamonn Maguire, Robert S. Laramee, Helwig Hauser, Matthew Ward, and Min Chen, "Glyph-Based Visualization: Foundations, Design Guidelines, Techniques and Applications," paper presented at Eurographics 2013, Girona, Spain, May 6–10, 2013. As of August 22, 2018:
http://www.cs.swan.ac.uk/~csbob/research/star/glyph/borgo13glyph7feb.pdf

Bose, Indranil, and Radha K. Mahapatra, "Business Data Mining—A Machine Learning Perspective," *Information & Management*, Vol. 39, No. 3, December 2001, pp. 211–225. As of September 21, 2017:
http://www.sciencedirect.com/science/article/pii/S037872060100091X

Boyd, Curtis, "The Future of MISO," *Special Warfare*, Vol. 24, No. 1, January–February 2011, pp. 22–29. As of September 21, 2017:
https://www.dvidshub.net/publication/issues/8092

Brady, Henry E., and David Collier, *Rethinking Social Inquiry: Diverse Tools, Shared Standards*, Lanham, Md.: Rowman & Littlefield Publishers, 2004.

Brown, Ryan A., David P. Kennedy, Joan S. Tucker, Daniela Golinelli, and Suzanne L. Wenzel, "Monogamy on the Street: A Mixed-Methods Study of Homeless Men," *Journal of Mixed Methods Research*, Vol. 7, No. 4, October 2013. As of July 26, 2018:
http://journals.sagepub.com/doi/pdf/10.1177/1558689813480000

Chatterjee, Samprit, and Ali S. Hadi, *Sensitivity Analysis in Linear Regression*, Hoboken, N.J.: John Wiley & Sons, 2009.

Checchi, Francesco, Barclay T. Stewart, Jennifer J. Palmer, and Chris Grundy, "Validity and Feasibility of a Satellite Imagery-Based Method for Rapid Estimation of Displaced Populations," *International Journal of Health Geographics*, Vol. 12, No. 4, January 23, 2013. As of September 21, 2017:
https://doi.org/10.1186/1476-072X-12-4

Collier, David, "Understanding Process Tracing," *Political Science & Politics*, Vol. 44, No. 4, October 2011, pp. 823–830. As of July 24, 2018:
https://www.cambridge.org/core/journals/ps-political-science-and-politics/article/understanding-process-tracing/183A057AD6A36783E678CB37440346D1

Condra, Luke N., Joseph H. Felter, Radha K. Iyengar, and Jacob N. Shapiro, "The Effect of Civilian Casualties in Afghanistan and Iraq," working paper, Cambridge, Mass.: National Bureau of Economic Research, 2010. As of July 26, 2018:
http://www.offnews.info/downloads/w16152.pdf

Connable, Ben, *Embracing the Fog of War: Assessment and Metrics in Counterinsurgency*, Santa Monica, Calif.: RAND Corporation, MG-1086-DOD, 2012. As of September 22, 2017:
https://www.rand.org/pubs/monographs/MG1086.html

Connable, Ben, Walter L. Perry, Abby Doll, Natasha Lander, and Dan Madden, *Modeling, Simulation, and Operations Analysis in Afghanistan and Iraq: Operational Vignettes, Lessons Learned, and a Survey of Selected Efforts*, Santa Monica, Calif.: RAND Corporation, RR-382-OSD, 2014. As of September 22, 2017: https://www.rand.org/pubs/research_reports/RR382.html

Creswell, John W., *Research Design: Qualitative, Quantitative, and Mixed Methods Approaches*, Thousand Oaks, Calif.: SAGE Publications, 2013.

Deployable Training Division, *Insights and Best Practices Focus Paper: Design and Planning*, Suffolk, Va.: Joint Staff J7, July 2013. As of August 22, 2018: http://www.jcs.mil/Portals/36/Documents/Doctrine/fp/design_and_planning_fp.pdf

Egel, Daniel, and Peter Glick, *Assessing the Stabilizing Effects of Development Programming: A Review of USAID's Evaluation Efforts in Afghanistan*, Santa Monica, Calif.: RAND Corporation, WR-1106-MSI, 2016. As of September 22, 2017: https://www.rand.org/pubs/working_papers/WR1106.html

Egel, Daniel, Charles P. Ries, Ben Connable, Todd C. Helmus, Eric Robinson, Isaac Baruffi, Melissa A. Bradley, Kurt Card, Kathleen Loa, Sean Mann, Fernando Sedano, Stephan B. Seabrook, and Robert Stewart, *Investing in the Fight: Assessing the Use of the Commander's Emergency Response Program in Afghanistan*, Santa Monica, Calif.: RAND Corporation, RR-1508-OSD, 2016. As of September 22, 2017: https://www.rand.org/pubs/research_reports/RR1508.html

Fearon, James, "Selection Effects and Deterrence," *International Interactions*, Vol. 28, No. 1, 2002, pp. 5–29.

Felter, Joseph H., *Taking Guns to a Knife Fight: Effective Military Support to COIN*, Carlisle Barracks, Pa.: Army War College, 2008. As of July 25, 2018: http://www.dtic.mil/dtic/tr/fulltext/u2/a510853.pdf

Field Manual 3-07.1, *Security Force Assistance*, Washington, D.C., Headquarters, Department of the Army, May 2009. As of August 28, 2018: https://www.press.umich.edu/pdf/9780472033904-FM3071.pdf

Field Manual 3-53, *Military Information Support Operations*, Washington, D.C.: Headquarters, U.S. Army, 2013.

Field Manual 6-99, *U.S. Army Report and Message Formats*, Washington, D.C.: Headquarters, Department of the Army, August 19, 2013. As of September 21, 2017: https://armypubs.army.mil/epubs/DR_pubs/DR_a/pdf/web/fm6_99.pdf

FM—*See* Field Manual.

Freedman, David, "From Association to Causation: Some Remarks on the History of Statistics," *Statistical Science*, Vol. 14, No. 3, August 1999, pp. 243–258.

Fridovich, David P., and Fred T. Krawchuk, "Winning in the Pacific: The Special Operations Forces Indirect Approach," *Joint Force Quarterly*, No. 44, 1st Quarter 2007, pp. 24–27. As of July 26, 2018:
http://ndupress.ndu.edu/portals/68/Documents/jfq/jfq-44.pdf

Gourley, Scott R., "The Four Pillars of Army SOF: Lt. Gen. Ken Tovo Describes USASOC Today," interview, *The Year in Special Operations 2017–2018*, 2017. As of September 24, 2018:
http://www.nxtbook.com/faircount/YISO/YISO17/index.php?startid=C1#/50

Greenley, Brendan, and Dave Ohls, "Countering Radicalization: An Agent-Based Model of Precision Strike Campaigns," paper, April 6, 2014. As of August 22, 2018:
https://brendangreenley.com/wp-content/uploads/2014/10/GreenleyOhlsMPSAPaper.pdf

Headquarters, Combined Joint Special Operations Task Force–Afghanistan, *Village Stability Operations and Afghan Local Police: Bottom-Up Counterinsurgency*, April 1, 2011.

Heatherly, Chris, and Elizabeth Molnar, *The Regional Command–East Regional Information Fusion Center (RIFC) in Afghanistan*, working paper, undated.

Hermon, Renuka, "Addressing Human Security Issues: Cause Award Honoree IST Research," June 16, 2017. As of August 22, 2018:
https://www.elastic.co/blog/addressing-human-security-issues-cause-award-honoree-ist-research

Hernandez, Alejandro S., Julian Ouellet, and Christopher J. Nannini, "Circular Logic and Constant Progress: IW Assessments in Afghanistan," in George W. Casey, Jr., Leo J. Blanken, Hy Rothstein, and Jason J. Lepore, eds., *Assessing War: The Challenge of Measuring Success and Failure*," Washington, D.C.: Georgetown University Press, 2015.

JDN—*See* Joint Doctrine Note.

Johnson, R. Burke, Anthony J. Onwuegbuzie, and Lisa A. Turner, "Toward a Definition of Mixed Methods Research," *Journal of Mixed Methods Research*, Vol. 1, No. 2, April 2007, pp. 112–133.

Johnston, Patrick B., and Anoop K. Sarbahi, "The Impact of US Drone Strikes on Terrorism in Pakistan," *International Studies Quarterly*, Vol. 60, No. 2, June 2016, pp. 203–219. As of September 21, 2017:
http://dx.doi.org/10.1093/isq/sqv004

Joint Doctrine Note 1-15, *Operation Assessment*, Washington, D.C.: Joint Staff, January 15, 2015.

Joint Publication 1-02, *DoD Dictionary of Military and Associated Terms*, Washington, D.C.: Joint Staff, August 2018. As of September 20, 2018: http://www.jcs.mil/Portals/36/Documents/Doctrine/pubs/dictionary.pdf?ver=2018-09-06-102155-910

Joint Publication 3-05, *Special Operations*, Washington, D.C.: Joint Chiefs of Staff, July 16, 2014.

Joint Publication 3-13.2, *Military Information Support Operations*, Washington, D.C.: Joint Chiefs of Staff, December 20, 2011, pp. I-2, 3

Joint Publication 3-57, *Civil-Military Operations*, Washington, D.C.: Joint Staff, September 11, 2013.

Joint Publication 5-0, *Joint Planning*, Washington, D.C.: Joint Chiefs of Staff, June 16, 2017. As of August 22, 2018:
http://www.jcs.mil/Portals/36/Documents/Doctrine/pubs/jp5_0_20171606.pdf

Joint Special Operations Task Force–Philippines, "JSOTF-P Overview," briefing slides, 2008.

Joint Staff, *Commander's Handbook for Assessment Planning and Execution*, Vers. 1.0, Suffolk, Va.: Joint Staff J-7, Joint and Coalition Warfighting, September 9, 2011. As of July 25, 2018:
http://www.jcs.mil/Portals/36/Documents/Doctrine/pams_hands/assessment_hbk.pdf

Joint Warfighting Center, *Commander's Handbook for Attack the Network*, Vers. 1.0, Suffolk, Va.: Joint Doctrine Support Division, 2011. As of September 24, 2018:
http://www.jcs.mil/Portals/36/Documents/Doctrine/pams_hands/atn_hbk.pdf

Jones, Seth G., Andrew Liepman, and Nathan Chandler, *Counterterrorism and Counterinsurgency in Somalia: Assessing the Campaign Against al Shabaab*, Santa Monica, Calif.: RAND Corporation, RR-1539-OSD, 2016. As of September 22, 2017:
https://www.rand.org/pubs/research_reports/RR1539.html

JP—*See* Joint Publication.

Kelley, Ninette, Peta Sandison, and Simon Lawry-White, *Enhancing UNHCR's Capacity to Monitor the Protection, Rights and Well-Being of Refugees*, Geneva: United Nations High Commissioner for Refugees Evaluation and Policy Analysis Unit, EPAU/2004/06, June 2004. As of July 25, 2018:
http://www.unhcr.org/40d9781d4.pdf

Khalil, James, "The Reliability of Perception Surveys in Afghanistan," University of Sussex Institute of Development Studies, HiCN Research Design Note 15, October 2012. As of July 25, 2018:
http://www.hicn.org/wordpress/wp-content/uploads/2012/06/HiCN-RDN-15.pdf

King, Gary, Robert O. Keohane, and Sidney Verba, *Designing Social Inquiry: Scientific Inference in Qualitative Research*, Princeton, N.J.: Princeton University Press, 1994.

Krizhevsky, Alexander, Ilya Sutskever, and Geoffrey E. Hinton, "System and Method for Generating Training Cases for Image Classification," U.S. Patent, February 2, 2016. As of August 28, 2018: https://patentimages.storage.googleapis.com/2c/66/cd/ffe937d9ffe545/US9251437.pdf

Li, Xi, and Deren Li, "Can Night-Time Light Images Play a Role in Evaluating the Syrian Crisis?" *International Journal of Remote Sensing*, Vol. 35, No. 18, 2014, pp. 6648–6661. As of September 21, 2017: http://dx.doi.org/10.1080/01431161.2014.971469

Long, Austin, Stephanie Pezard, Bryce Loidolt, and Todd C. Helmus, *Locals Rule: Historical Lessons for Creating Local Defense Forces for Afghanistan and Beyond*, Santa Monica, Calif.: RAND Corporation, MG-1232-CFSOCC-A, 2012. As of September 22, 2017: https://www.rand.org/pubs/monographs/MG1232.html

Marquis, Jefferson P., Michael J. McNerney, S. Rebecca Zimmerman, Merrie Archer, Jeremy Boback, and Dave Stebbins, *Developing an Assessment, Monitoring, and Evaluation Framework for U.S. Department of Defense Security Cooperation*, Santa Monica, Calif.: RAND Corporation, RR-1611-OSD, 2016. As of September 22, 2017: https://www.rand.org/pubs/research_reports/RR1611.html

Mueller, John E., "The Search for the 'Breaking Point' in Vietnam: The Statistics of a Deadly Quarrel," *International Studies Quarterly*, Vol. 24, No. 4, December 1980, pp. 497–519.

Mushen, Emily and Jonathan Schroden, *Are We Winning? A Brief History of Military Operations Assessment*, Washington, D.C.: CNA, September 2014.

Ong, Eileen Y. L., Rebecca P. Ang, Jim C. M. Ho, Joylynn C. Y. Lim, Dion H. Goh, Chei Sian Lee, and Alton Y. K. Chua, "Narcissism, Extraversion and Adolescents' Self-Presentation on Facebook," *Personality and Individual Differences*, Vol. 50, No. 2, January 2011, pp. 180–185. As of September 21, 2017: http://www.sciencedirect.com/science/article/pii/S0191886910004654

Osburg, Jan, Christopher Paul, Lisa Saum-Manning, Dan Madden, and Leslie Adrienne Payne, *Assessing Locally Focused Stability Operations*, Santa Monica, Calif.: RAND Corporation, RR-387-A, 2014. As of September 22, 2017: https://www.rand.org/pubs/research_reports/RR387.html

Paruchabutr, Gittipong, Christopher Parapone, Geoffrey Demarest, Grant Martin, Christopher Kirk, Cody Brown, Curtis Clayton, William Harris, Thomas Heilman, and Brian Kaiser, *SOF Campaign Planner's Handbook of Operational Art and Design*, Fort Bragg, N.C.: U.S. Army Special Operations Command, September 16, 2014.

Patton, Michael Quinn, "Enhancing the Quality and Credibility of Qualitative Analysis," *Health Services Research*, Vol. 34, No. 5, Pt. 2, December 1999, pp. 1189–1208. As of September 21, 2017:
http://www.ncbi.nlm.nih.gov/pmc/articles/PMC1089059/

Paul, Christopher, *Assessing and Evaluating Department of Defense Efforts to Inform, Influence, and Persuade: Worked Example*, Santa Monica, Calif.: RAND Corporation, RR-809/4-OSD, 2017. As of December 18, 2017:
https://www.rand.org/pubs/research_reports/RR809z4.html

Paul, Christopher, Colin P. Clarke, and Beth Grill, *Victory Has a Thousand Fathers: Sources of Success in Counterinsurgency*, Santa Monica, Calif.: RAND Corporation, MG-964-OSD, 2010. As of September 22, 2017:
https://www.rand.org/pubs/monographs/MG964.html

Paul, Christopher, Brian J. Gordon, Jennifer D. P. Moroney, Lisa Saum-Manning, Beth Grill, Colin P. Clarke, and Heather Peterson, *A Building Partner Capacity Assessment Framework: Tracking Inputs, Outputs, Outcomes, Disrupters, and Workarounds*, Santa Monica, Calif.: RAND Corporation, RR-935-OSD, 2015. As of September 22, 2017:
https://www.rand.org/pubs/research_reports/RR935.html

Paul, Christopher, Jessica Yeats, Colin P. Clarke, and Miriam Matthews, *Assessing and Evaluating Department of Defense Efforts to Inform, Influence, and Persuade: Desk Reference*, Santa Monica, Calif.: RAND Corporation, RR-809/1-OSD, 2015. As of September 22, 2017:
https://www.rand.org/pubs/research_reports/RR809z1.html

Perry, Walter L., Brian McInnis, Carter C. Price, Susan C. Smith, and John S. Hollywood, *Predicative Policing: The Role of Crime Forecasting in Law Enforcement Operations*, Santa Monica, Calif.: RAND Corporation, RR-233-NIJ, 2013. As of September 22, 2017:
https://www.rand.org/pubs/research_reports/RR233.html

Petit, Brian, "The Fight for the Village: Southern Afghanistan, 2010," *Military Review*, May–June 2011.

Rabinowitz, Nicholas, "The OCHA Sitrep: Open Access and Political Pressure in Humanitarian Information," master's thesis, Berkeley, Calif.: University of California, Berkeley, May 7, 2009.

Raleigh, Clionadh, and Caitriona Dowd, "Armed Conflict Location and Event Data Project (ACLED) Codebook," Armed Conflict Location and Event Data Project website, 2015. As of September 21, 2017: http://www.acleddata.com/wp-content/uploads/2015/01/ACLED_Codebook_2015.pdf

Robinson, Linda, *The Future of U.S. Special Operations Forces*, Washington, D.C.: Council on Foreign Relations, 2013. As of September 21, 2017: http://www.cfr.org/special-operations/future-us-special-operations-forces/p30323

Robinson, Linda, *Assessment of the Politico-Military Campaign to Counter ISIL and Options for Adaptation*, Santa Monica, Calif.: RAND Corporation, RR-1290-OSD, 2016. As of September 22, 2017: https://www.rand.org/pubs/research_reports/RR1290.html

Robinson, Linda, Daniel Egel, and Ryan Andrew Brown, *Measuring the Effectiveness of Special Operations: Appendixes*, Santa Monica, Calif.: RAND Corporation, RR-2504/1-A, 2019. As of October 2019: https://www.rand.org/pubs/research_reports/RR2504.html

Robinson, Linda, Patrick B. Johnston, and Gillian S. Oak, *U.S. Special Operations Forces in the Philippines, 2001–2014*, Santa Monica, Calif.: RAND Corporation, RR-1236-OSD, 2016. As of September 22, 2017: https://www.rand.org/pubs/research_reports/RR1236.html

Romero, Adriana, Carlo Gatta, and Gustau Camps-Valls, "Unsupervised Deep Feature Extraction for Remote Sensing Image Classification," *IEEE Transactions on Geoscience and Remote Sensing*, Vol. 54, No. 3, 2016, pp. 1349–1362.

Rosello, Victor M., "Lessons from El Salvador," *Parameters*, Vol. 23, Winter 1993–1994, pp. 100–108.

Russakovsky, Olga, Jia Deng, Hao Su, Jonathan Krause, Sanjeev Satheesh, Sean Ma, Zhiheng Huang, Andrej Karpathy, Aditya Khosla, Michael Bernstein, Alexander C. Berg, and Li Fei-Fei, "ImageNet Large Scale Visual Recognition Challenge," *International Journal of Computer Vision*, Vol. 115, No. 3, 2015, pp. 211–252. As of September 21, 2017: http://dx.doi.org/10.1007/s11263-015-0816-y

Schroden, Jonathan, "Why Operations Assessments Fail: It's Not Just the Metrics," *Naval War College Review*, Vol. 64, No. 4, Autumn 2011, pp. 89–102.

Shelton, Henry H., "Special Operations Forces: Key Role in Preventive Defense," *DISAM Journal*, Summer 1997, pp. 55–57. As of July 27, 2018: http://www.disam.dsca.mil/Pubs/Indexes/Vol%2019_4/SOF.pdf

Slider, Jason, "95th Civil Affairs Brigade Capabilities," slide, Fort Bragg, N.C.: U.S. Army Special Operations Command, 2017.

Sopko, John F., "Assessing the Capabilities and Effectiveness of the Afghan National Defense and Security Forces," testimony before the Subcommittee on Oversight and Investigations, Committee on Armed Services, U.S. House of Representatives, February 12, 2016.

Sotire, Robert B., "Measuring Performance and Effectiveness in Irregular Warfare: Preventing Dysfunctional Behavior," Newport, R.I.: Naval War College, 2009.

Steelberg, Ryan, and Chad Steelberg, "Engine and System for the Transcription and Assessment of Media Files," U.S. Patent Application Publication, February 23, 2017. As of August 28, 2018:
https://patentimages.storage.googleapis.com/3b/ee/74/31c70e06c13b9e/US20170053323A1.pdf

Strobl, Carolin, James Malley, and Gerhard Tutz, "An Introduction to Recursive Partitioning: Rationale, Application, and Characteristics of Classification and Regression Trees, Bagging, and Random Forests," *Psychological Methods*, Vol. 14, No. 4, December 2009, pp. 323–348.

Sweetland, Anders, *Item Analysis of the HES (Hamlet Evaluation System)*, Santa Monica, Calif.: RAND Corporation, D-17634-ARPA/AGILE, 1968. As of September 22, 2017:
https://www.rand.org/pubs/documents/D17634.html

SynGlyphX, "Syria: Crisis in Context," video, 2017. As of July 27, 2018:
https://www.youtube.com/watch?v=yfVe7HZnBt8

Tien, James M., "Big Data: Unleashing Information," *Journal of Systems Science and Systems Engineering*, Vol. 22, No. 2, June 1, 2013, pp. 127–151.

Tucker, David, and Christopher J. Lamb, *United States Special Operations Forces*, New York: Columbia University Press, 2007.

Tufekci, Zeynep, "Big Questions for Social Media Big Data: Representativeness, Validity and Other Methodological Pitfalls," *Proceedings of the Eighth International AAAI Conference on Weblogs and Social Media*, 2014, pp. 505–514. As of July 27, 2018:
https://www.aaai.org/ocs/index.php/ICWSM/ICWSM14/paper/view/8062/8151

Tufekci, Zeynep, and Christopher Wilson, "Social Media and the Decision to Participate in Political Protest: Observations from Tahrir Square," *Journal of Communication*, Vol. 62, No. 2, 2012, pp. 363–379

United Nations Office on Drugs and Crime, "Criminal Justice Assessment Toolkit," webpage, 2006. As of December 21, 2017:
https://www.unodc.org/unodc/en/justice-and-prison-reform/Criminal-Justice-Toolkit.html

Upshur, William P., Jonathon W. Roginski, and David J. Kilcullen, "Recognizing Systems in Afghanistan: Lessons Learned and New Approaches to Operational Assessments," *Prism*, Vol. 3, No. 3, June 2012, pp. 87–104.

U.S. Army, "Warrior Forge 2012: The Road to War," 2012. As of September 21, 2017:
https://www.usm.edu/sites/default/files/groups/army-rotc/pdf/common_teaching_senario_road_to_war.pdf

U.S. Army Special Operations Command, *Communicating the ARSOF Narrative and Setting the Course to 2035*, Fort Bragg, Calif.: John F. Kennedy Special Warfare Center and School, 2017a.

U.S. Army Special Operations Command, "Designation of Psychological Operations Units Assigned to the United States Army Special Operations Command," memorandum for the record, October 27, 2017b.

U.S. Army War College, *Campaign Planning Handbook*, Carlisle Barracks, Pa.: Department of Military Strategy, Planning, and Operations, 2016.

USASOC—*See* U.S. Army Special Operations Command.

U.S. Code Title 10, §167, Unified Combatant Command for Special Operations Forces, as of January 3, 2012. As of August 22, 2018:
https://www.gpo.gov/fdsys/search/pagedetails.action?packageId=USCODE-2011-title10&granuleId=USCODE-2011-title10-subtitleA-partI-chap6-sec167

U.S. Government Accountability Office, *Security Assistance: Evaluations Needed to Determine Effectiveness of U.S. Aid to Lebanon's Security Forces*, Washington, D.C., GAO-13-289, March 19, 2013. As of July 26, 2018:
https://www.gao.gov/products/GAO-13-289

U.S. Joint Forces Command, *Commander's Handbook for Joint Battle Damage Assessment*, Joint Warfighting Center, June 1, 2004. As of September 21, 2017:
http://www.dtic.mil/doctrine/doctrine/jwfc/hbk_jbda.pdf

U.S. Special Operations Command, *Fact Book 2013*, Tampa, Fla., 2013.

Vogel, Isabel, *Review of the Use of 'Theory of Change' in International Development*, UK Department of International Development, April 2012. As of July 26, 2018:
http://www.theoryofchange.org/pdf/DFID_ToC_Review_VogelV7.pdf

Weller, Susan C., "Cultural Consensus Theory: Applications and Frequently Asked Questions," *Field Methods*, Vol. 19, No. 4, November 1, 2007, pp. 339–368. As of September 21, 2017:
http://fmx.sagepub.com/cgi/content/abstract/19/4/339

White, Susan S., Rose A. Mueller-Hanson, David W. Dorsey, Elaine D. Pulakos, Michelle M. Wisecarver, Edwin A. Deagle III, and Kip G. Mendini, *Developing Adaptive Proficiency in Special Forces Officers*, Arlington, Va.: U.S. Army Research Institute for the Behavioral and Social Sciences, 2005.

Woolley, Samuel C., "Automating Power: Social Bot Interference in Global Politics," *First Monday*, Vol. 21, No. 4, April 2016.

World Bank, *Results Framework and M&E Guidance Note*, April 9, 2013. As of July 27, 2018:
http://siteresources.worldbank.org/PROJECTS/Resources/40940-1365611011935/Guidance_Note_Results_and_M&E.pdf

World Bank, "Software for Poverty Mapping," August 11, 2016. As of August 28, 2018:
http://www.worldbank.org/en/research/brief/software-for-poverty-mapping

Worthan, Shannon R., "Assessing the Impact of Information Channels on the Understanding of Ground Truth," master's thesis, Monterey, Calif.: Naval Postgraduate School, 2012.

Zhao, Ying, Douglas J. MacKinnon, and Shelley P. Gallup, "System Self-Awareness and Related Methods for Improving the Use and Understanding of Data Within DoD," *Software Quality Professional*, Vol. 13, No. 4, September 2011, pp. 19–31.

Zheng, Li, Chao Shen, Liang Tang, Chunqiu Zeng, Tao Li, Steve Luis, Shu-Ching Chen, and Jainendra K. Navlakha, "Disaster SITREP—A Vertical Search Engine and Information Analysis Tool in Disaster Management Domain," presented at the 2012 IEEE 13th International Conference on Information Reuse and Integration (IRI), August 8–10, 2012, pp. 457–465.